DEMCO

INDUSTRIAL POLLUTION:

POISONING OUR PLANET

INDUSTRIAL POLLUTION: POISONING OUR PLANET

BY
EVE AND ALBERT STWERTKA

A GROLIER COMPANY

FRANKLIN WATTS
NEW YORK | LONDON | TORONTO | SYDNEY | 1981
AN IMPACT BOOK

ACKNOWLEDGMENTS

The authors are grateful for help and information
extended by the Environmental Defense Fund,
the U.S. Environmental Protection Agency (EPA),
and the *Niagara Gazette* of Niagara Falls, New York.

Our special thanks go to Dr. Howard Beim, Professor
of Chemistry, United States Merchant Marine Academy,
Kings Point, whose expertise proved of great value
in the preparation of this book.

Library of Congress Cataloging in Publication Data

Stwertka, Eve.
Industrial pollution.

(An Impact book)
Bibliography: p.
Includes index.
SUMMARY: Discusses the horrible effects of industrial pollution and industrial waste on human beings
and their environment.
1. Pollution—Juvenile literature.   2.   Factory and
trade waste—Juvenile literature.   [1.   Pollution.
2.   Factory and trade waste]   I.   Stwertka, Albert,
joint author.   II.   Title.
TD176.S85   363.73   80-25898
ISBN 0-531-04261-8

6 5

FOR STELLA AND ERNST

CONTENTS

INDUSTRIAL POLLUTION:

POISONING OUR PLANET

CHAPTER I
INDUSTRY—
OUR NEIGHBOR

A cloud of white poison spreads its blight across a peaceful countryside; a stew of chemical wastes oozes into private homes; thousands of barrels of oil spill into the oceans; radioactive gases escape into the air. These are only a few of the recent assaults on our planet earth caused by poor handling of hazardous industrial materials. Today, wherever scientists turn to investigate, they find contaminated wildlife, fish, water, and foodstuff.

The effects on human health have been devastating. Researchers are discovering that exposure to certain substances can cause painful, disfiguring, or even fatal diseases. Exposure can cause many types of cancer. It may be responsible for causing young men to become sterile and young women to have miscarriages or to bear children with birth defects. In other words, our surroundings contain pollutants that are toxic (poisonous), carcinogenic (cancer producing), mutagenic (capable of causing hereditary changes), and teratogenic (capable of causing malformed births).

NEW FORMS OF
AN ANCIENT PROBLEM

Pollution is not a new problem, of course. It existed in ancient Rome, plagued cities in the Middle Ages, and grew much worse after the start of the Industrial Revolution. In the twentieth century, pollution has turned out to be the dark side of brilliant new engineering feats such as the utilization of petroleum for new products and the release of energy by splitting atoms.

Our ancestors could hardly have imagined the enormous quantity and variety of our industrial output or the massive side effects and sheer tonnage of waste it produces. More important still, they would have been surprised by the basic difference in quality between certain pollutants today and those of the past. Modern technology has devised new materials whose impact on our surroundings is pervasive, stubborn, and complex.

Each year, several thousand new chemicals are added to the American market. Many of these substances hold unknown dangers. But neither the manufacturer nor any government agency has enough time and resources to test them all thoroughly. Besides, many substances are so useful that they are needed in spite of the danger they present.

The chemical industry, the petroleum industry, and the nuclear industry together produce an array of substances that are intended to help us but that can become our deadly foes. When technologists capture natural forces and put them to work, they sometimes overlook the destructive powers they may be releasing.

WORLD WAR
AND TECHNOLOGY

Why the sudden upsurge of so many harmful new products? World War II, which America joined in 1941 and which ended in 1945, stimulated a great deal of industrial growth. First of all, a search was on to develop new weapons of warfare; then, there was a shortage of natural raw materials such as metal, wood, wool, and cotton, which created the need for new synthetic substances. Thus the plastics industry was born. When the war ended, many devastated regions needed rebuilding and their inhabitants had to be kept from starvation. More grain, milk, meat, and fruit were needed to support a hungry world. Scientists and technicians came up with new chemicals to wipe out agricultural pests, to destroy weeds, to fertilize farm land, and to fatten cattle and poultry.

America sent many goods and services to other countries. At home, newly developed products created new industries and gave people good jobs and money to spend. Americans not only built new factories, but they also built housing developments and shopping centers, cut roads through the countryside, bought cars by the billions, and gave birth to record numbers of children. Soon, these children were themselves in need of more food, clothing, houses, stores, roads, cars, and consumer products. As families grew, and as workers immigrated from abroad to take jobs that needed filling, the population of the United States rose dramatically. The number of people in America nearly doubled from 132 million in 1940 to 222 million in 1980. As for the population of the entire world, it doubled from 2 billion in 1950 to 4 billion in 1980.

Everyone was buying, everyone was producing. People wanted beef and milk on their tables daily, and that necessitated pesticides and chemical fertilizers for the farms. People wanted radios and TV and hi-fi sets with casings made of plastic. People wanted wash-and-wear polyester shirts, nylon tents, fiberglass boats, and myriad other products using the complex new chemistry developed during the war. They wanted cars, trucks, and planes fueled by petroleum. They wanted clean, efficient oil heat for their houses. And the factories, which multiplied in number to make all these products, needed energy and more energy to run them. Even though we Americans make up less than 6 percent of the world's population, we now consume more than 30 percent of the world's energy. The United States has also long been the largest consumer of the world's petroleum. Thus it became necessary to supplement our energy resources by means of one more new product of postwar ingenuity: nuclear power plants.

DANGEROUS FORCES

Humans have always struggled for power over nature, beginning with early times when they harnessed fire and found medical uses for certain poisons. Awesome forces and deadly substances have been made to serve us well. They must be watched and controlled constantly, though. As our technology becomes more and more complex, we find it more and more difficult to keep track of all its aspects. The result may be disaster.

Hazardous materials can never be left without supervision. They pose a threat from the moment they are manufactured to the time when they are no longer needed and must somehow be destroyed. They are dangerous to store and dangerous to transport. Coping with their waste products often presents the biggest headache of all.

Hazardous materials in a gaseous state can quickly disperse into the surroundings or they can explode. Liquid materials, too, can explode and cause huge fires. They can corrode their containers and leak out to soak into the ground and seep into water supplies. Tank cars and trucks carrying chemicals frequently derail and overturn, emptying their contents over the countryside. Underwater oil wells blow out during drilling, blighting sea life and polluting beaches. Oil-carrying tankers can become leaking wrecks.

The atomic power industry has its own special problems. Aside from the constant need to monitor radioactive emissions from power plants, there is the question of uranium transportation and the problem of waste disposal. How can one safely discard the tailings or debris of uranium mines? How can one get rid of thousands of gallons of radioactive water or a battery of spent uranium fuel rods?

How can one safely dismantle an entire nuclear power plant that has outlived its usefulness?

Poorly planned dumping of wastes at random disposal sites has polluted soil, rivers, lakes, and oceans. Toxic substances enter our food and drink and eventually even appear in the milk of nursing mothers.

It also happens that by sheer carelessness in handling and storage, poisonous chemicals are substituted for beneficial ones. In the early 1970s, a fire retardant was inadvertently added to dairy cattle feed in the state of Michigan. Hundreds of cows died or had to be destroyed. Even so, the fire retardant, having contaminated milk, meat, and eggs, was consumed by most Michigan residents as well as many outsiders.

MORE ENEMIES

Occasionally, too, scientists discover hazards springing from materials that are neither explosive, nor poisonous, nor corrosive, nor radioactive. Asbestos is such a material. It is useful as a fire retardant in building materials and household utensils; but its dust is easily inhaled, stays lodged in the body, and slowly causes irreparable damage.

Similarly, new discoveries were recently made about a group of inert gases called fluorocarbons. In compressed form, fluorocarbons were long used to power many different kinds of spray cans, and they are still widely used as refrigerants. Freed from compression, fluorocarbons rise to the earth's upper atmosphere. There they lodge and slowly destroy the ozone layer that protects our globe from ultraviolet radiation. The result is likely to be a higher incidence of skin cancers in humans. The loss of ozone may also cause changes in plant growth and in the earth's climate.

Some of the most harmful materials, of course, are those manufactured for warfare or national defense. From the start, their purpose is destruction. Defoliants and nerve gases are a dangerous hoard to keep and to transport. Nuclear weapons, even those detonated only for testing, leave traces of radioactive fallout worldwide. During the bomb testing of the 1950s and 1960s, even milk was contaminated by radioactive isotopes.

DANGEROUS WORK

The first people to be hurt by hazardous materials are the workers who come in close daily contact with them. Sad to say, these workers serve as guinea pigs to alert us to danger. This was certainly true of some of the early nuclear scientists who carelessly handled seemingly harmless radium. Many of them developed cancer or other radiation-induced diseases.

Workers in chemical factories are exposed to great danger. Exposure to vinyl chloride, for example, leads to a high incidence of bladder cancer. Exposure to many types of pesticides causes cancer of the liver. Exposure to benzene has been proved to cause leukemia. Inhaling asbestos fibers induces fatal lung disease. In many cases, young chemical workers have found themselves sterile or have been grieved to see their children stillborn or malformed.

The Occupational Safety and Health Administration has recently prepared a list of 2,500 suspected carcinogens to be regulated in the work place. Of these, five hundred are candidates for immediate regulation. The agency will use this list to require industries to protect their workers. This could be done by improved safety engineering and by shorter periods of work exposure. These chemicals may some day be banned entirely, if substitutes for them can be found.

Without certain hazardous materials, though, our modern world would be unmanageable. Chemical fertilizers, pesticides, and disinfectants save us from starvation and from diseases, such as cholera, typhus, malaria, and the bubonic plague which wiped out a quarter of the population of Europe in the fourteenth century. If we want to feed, clothe, house, and transport our still-increasing world population and if we want to improve living standards in regions where people suffer from hunger, industrial countries will have to continue producing many kinds of hazardous materials.

Strictly speaking, hazardous materials surround us everywhere, even in our homes. Medications, household cleansers, food additives, insulating materials, insect sprays, plant fertilizers, and automotive fuels all have the power to poison us. Most people are limited in their freedom to choose which of these products and how many they want to take into their lives.

In this book we will not concentrate on those hazardous materials that reach us in small quantities and which we can, to some extent, control. Our book will report on materials which can break out of restraint in large quantities and which threaten to enter our lives destructively, as huge impersonal forces that we cannot escape.

CHAPTER II
DISASTER FROM THE SKIES

In northern Italy the July sun is brilliant at midday. It was a perfect day for swimming. Paolo and Angela Venturi (let us call them that to preserve their privacy) were only waiting out the required hour after lunch before running to meet their friends at the community pool.

Angela, soon to be sixteen, and her thirteen-year-old brother were busy in the garden near the rabbit cages, filling a basket with grass clippings for their five white charges. Their dog Yip, always eager for attention, tumbled about their feet in a shower of fresh-cut grass. They had just picked up the basket when a sudden noise—a deep, gigantic rumbling—startled them into setting it down again.

With Yip barking at their heels they ran towards the house just as their mother hastened out to find them. All three stood still, looking at the sky.

Within a few minutes they noted a massive whitish cloud over the community of Meda, somewhat north of their own town of Seveso. It did not look like an ordinary cloud but was shaped something like an ice cream cone turned upside down. As they watched, it came rapidly nearer. All at once, a thick fog surrounded the little group and a fine snow of moist white crystals came sifting down. A choking odor of chemicals made the children gasp for air. Horrified, their eyes tearing, their skin damp, they rushed into the house and closed all doors and windows.

On Paolo's watch, the time read 12:45. "This stuff looks clean, but it smells awful," he complained. "We'd better shower and change our clothes," his mother said. Later on, she was grateful for her impulse.

Seveso, where Angela and Paolo had lived all their lives, is situated near the great industrial city, Milan. Parts of this ancient region of Lombardy are still rich in small farms and fruit orchards. The homes of Seveso are surrounded by gardens. The inhabitants were used to growing their own fruits and vegetables. In addition, many families liked to keep a few chickens, rabbits, and ducks for their family table.

In recent years, though, more and more factories had been springing up throughout the territory. Often, the air was hazy with industrial fumes. One factory in particular, seemed to emit unusually acrid odors. That was the ICMESA chemical plant, a subsidiary of an international chemical, cosmetics, and drug concern. The name, an Italian acronym, stands for Chemical Industries of Meda, Incorporated. ICMESA was engaged in manufacturing some of the basic ingredients for cosmetics, among them a substance called trichlorophenol (TCP). TCP is used in making a disinfectant, or bactericide, called hexachlorophene and also a weed killer, or herbicide, called 2,4,5,-T.

Both hexachlorophene and 2,4,5,-T had recently come under suspicion of being hazardous to human health. In the United States, hexachlorophene had been marketed in deodorant soaps and other skin cleansers. It was used in homes, hospitals, and laundries. The weed killer 2,4,5,-T was also in widespread use, though it, too, had become suspect of causing health damage by the time of the ICMESA accident—July 10, 1976.

In the community of Meda, the ICMESA factory's close neighbors had long accommodated themselves to the odors. In fact, it had happened now and then that one of their rabbits or chickens had died a sudden mysterious death. On these occasions, they would take the dead animal to the factory office where someone would quickly and quietly pay them a small sum of money for their loss. No one had ever lodged an official complaint.

On this particular Saturday morning, the ICMESA plant was closed. For some reason, though, a series of chemical reactions, usually completed before the factory shut down for the weekend, had not been finished on the previous day. None of the plant's operators realized that inside the locked building a chemical mixture had been left heating in its huge tank. The temperature rose all night and all morning. Shortly after noon, the mixture—tetrachloro-benzene and sodium hydroxide in a solvent of ethylene glycol—boiled up and exploded. It blew out a safety valve and mounted through a venting tube. Then, rumbling and hissing, it spurted into the sky.

The monstrous white plume that shot out of confinement gathered into a cloud. Caught by the wind, it drifted south, and, as it cooled, it softly released its shower of white poison over a cone-shaped area of land. It drifted over a large part of Seveso and continued over the communities of Cesano, Maderno, and Desio. As yet, no one knew that the white crystals, which soon dissolved into an oily coating on leaves, fruit, roofs, and grass, were deadly.

After Paolo and Angela had showered and changed, they felt reluctant to go to the pool. But the afternoon was warm and many children did go to the pool in which the white crystals had quickly dissolved. They swam in the water even though it felt slightly oily, and afterwards they tumbled on grass which had acquired a strange, glossy sheen.

Alerted to the accident, an engineer from ICMESA arrived at the plant a few hours later. He was not certain what had actually occurred. All the same, he called on the homes closest to the factory grounds and advised the owners not to eat fruit from their trees. It seemed, as he told people, that a kind of weed killer had escaped from the plant. A little further away, though, when evening came, the townspeople picked their fruit and vegetables for dinner, as usual, and brought them to the table.

On Sunday morning, Angela heard Paolo calling her from the garden. He wanted to show her the strange behavior of the neighbor's orange cat. Like someone drunk on alcohol, the cat was walking sideways, staggering, and falling over every few steps. Pursued by Yip's barking, the animal barely managed to creep into the hedge.

On their way to the rabbit cages, the children found a dead bird on the ground. Frightened now, they quickly tipped the rabbits' grass ration into the cages and returned to the house. Here, the phone was ringing as call after call came in. Friends and neighbors were concerned. Everyone had found dead birds and field mice in the gardens and on the streets.

Worse was to come. By Monday, many children and adults were feeling ill. Their heads were aching, their eyes were swollen. Many of them were nauseated and dizzy and some had diarrhea. Across the street from the Venturis, five-year-old Irma's face and arms had broken out in a red rash. In the doctor's office where her mother took her the next day, other parents were waiting with children whose skin was covered with the same burning sores.

Early on Wednesday, Mr. Venturi, driving along the tree-lined road on his way to work, noticed that the leaves, yellow and crumpled, had begun to fall. At about the same time, his wife was discovering the damage in the garden: blackened lettuces, rusty shrubbery. Near the rabbit cages she stopped, fearing what she might find. Indeed, only two of the rabbits were still alive. Blood trickling from their mouths stained the white fur. The other three lay dead.

By the end of the week, nineteen children, covered with large running sores, had been rushed to the hospital. And still, no one in authority had been able to identify the white poison that had sifted down over Seveso.

It took nine days after the explosion for scientists at the nearby Mario Negri Institute for pharmacological research

Two Seveso policemen patrol a road blocked by authorities inside the area contaminated by dioxin in 1976.

to discover the dreadful truth. In haste, they had searched their library for any technical literature published on the manufacturing history of trichlorophenol (TCP). They found that a few accidents had indeed occurred, here and there, over the last thirty years. The scientists noted that a radical transformation could occur in TCP when it became heated to above 200 degrees Centigrade (about 400 degrees Fahrenheit). Heating would turn some of its impurities into a new, far deadlier substance named tetrachlorodibenzo-p-dioxin (TCDD) usually called dioxin, for short. Whereas one gram of trichlorophenol mixed with 2 pounds (.90 kg) of rabbit food is likely to kill half the rabbits who eat it, it would merely take one-millionth of a gram of dioxin in the mixture to kill the same number of rabbits.

Complex modern instruments are needed to detect the presence and quantity of dioxin in matter. Fortunately, the Mario Negri Institute was equipped for the sophisticated and time-consuming techniques of gas chromatography and mass spectrometry. A few anguished days of working around the clock, and the worst suspicions were confirmed. Sometime in the early hours of July 10, a large quantity of dioxin—about 5 pounds (2 to 3 kg), if not more—was produced in the big heating tank of the ICMESA factory. For over a week dioxin had been lying on the community's roofs and gardens, on the soil, on people's clothes, and in their food.

TRICHLOROPHENOL

The discovery that a chemical is more dangerous than originally expected is usually made through illness among the workers who come in close contact with it. In the production of trichlorophenol several grave accidents had occurred in factories in the United States, Germany, England, and Holland as early as 1939. Typically, workers involved in these accidents developed chloracne, a skin disease showing reddish-black lesions or sores that can eventually cover the entire body and grow to egg-sized abscesses. These symptoms last for years and there is no known cure. It happened in some cases that the wives and children of workers, and even their household pets, developed chloracne from traces of the poison carried home on skin and clothes after a factory accident. Even worse, many workers sustained liver, kidney, and heart damage, bronchitis, infections of the sinus and tonsils, internal ulcerations, and hemorrhages. Some victims suffered from loss of hearing, smell, and taste or became partially paralyzed, drowsy, and uncoordinated. The worst cases ended in death.

Often it took only a very brief exposure for illness to occur. A young German bricklayer, for example, spent only two hours in the manufacturing area of a factory making TCDD. He developed severe chloracne. Within a year, he ran a high fever and developed a large bleeding tumor in his left lung. Another workman was sent to make repairs in a room that had been closed off and unused for four years after tri-chlorophenol had been manufactured there. Although he wore a suit of protective clothing, he several times removed his mask to wipe perspiration from his face. Only four days later, he developed chloracne and deafness. Within a few months he suffered a heart attack and while he was in the hospital a large painful tumor was found in his abdomen. After his death an autopsy showed ulceration of his intestines and liver as well as deterioration of fatty tissues in his body.

An explosion occurred in 1968 inside an English factory producing trichlorophenol. Seventy-nine workers, and even some members of their families, developed chloracne. Several workers died, primarily of liver damage. The contamination in the building was so persistent that the equipment had to be dismantled and buried deep in a former coal mine.

DEADLY COUSINS

Chemical compounds come in complicated "families." Most compounds have scores of chemical cousins whose makeup is similar but not precisely the same. Today, scientists using sophisticated instruments have begun to be able to separate seventy-five different chlorinated dioxins. Of these, the most toxic to laboratory animals, and probably also to humans, is 2,3,7,8-tetrachlorodibenzo-p-dioxin (2,3,7,8-TCDD). In reports written for the general public, the term dioxin is usually meant to designate this particular compound. Often, though, the term loosely covers the many different combinations in which 2,3,7,8-TCDD is found with some of the other seventy-four chlorinated dioxins.

Dioxin, in general, is a contaminant that occurs in the fabrication of many polychlorinated phenol products with a wide range of commercial uses. These products include wood-preservative fungicides and slime-killing agents in paper manufacture, in varnishes, paints, and adhesives, shampoos, soaps, and laundry agents.

From the start, when these products were first marketed in the late 1930s, accidents following their use were reported from various sources. The injuries reported ranged from chloracne in lumbermen using a wood preservative, to damage to unborn children, miscarriages, and the death of small infants.

In a St. Louis hospital, in 1969, two infants died and seven others barely survived. They had been diapered and clothed in linens laundered with a germicidal product containing pentachlorophenol. Later, even after the product was no longer used, traces of pentachlorophenol were still found in the blood of newborn babies and expectant mothers at the hospital. The toxin had clung to sheets and diapers even after several washings and had entered the bodies of mothers and babies through the skin.

Ten years later, hexachlorophenol was indicted in a study conducted in Sweden. Throughout their pregnancy, a group of young nurses and women doctors at a Swedish hospital had washed their hands with a liquid soap containing hexachlorophene. In keeping with hospital rules of hygiene, they had washed their hands as many as sixty to seventy times a day. Of 460 children born to them, 25 were severely malformed and 46 had minor deformities, a far larger percentage than that which occurred in a corresponding control group.

In America, hexachlorophene was widely used and advertised under the trade name PhisoHex as a cosmetic product for relieving adolescent acne. Late in the 1970s, though, its use was restricted to special applications in hospital surgery, and it is no longer available on the open drugstore shelf.

AGENT ORANGE

Perhaps the most controversial of the polychlorinated compounds is the weed killer 2,4,5-T. Under the official name of Agent Orange, it was used as a defoliant during the war in Vietnam. From 1962 to 1971, American armed forces sprayed 10.5 million gallons (39.75 million l) of it from low-flying helicopters over jungles where enemy troops were hiding their installations. Now, some years later, numerous Vietnam veterans appear to be experiencing a range of maladies which they attribute to the chemical's effects. A lawsuit by several thousand veterans has been brought against the five major American chemical companies manufacturing Agent Orange. The companies, in turn, disclaiming responsibility, have charged the government with improper handling.

At home, in peacetime, though, 2,4,5-T has found widespread use in forest management and agriculture. In the 1970s, a group of young women and their families, living in sparsely settled areas of Oregon, experienced a disaster from the sky all their own. A study there linked the high incidence of miscarriages among these women to the regular spraying of the weed killer from the air on surrounding timberlands.

A long-term study of Swedish railroad workers reported similar conclusions in 1979. Among several hundred employees who had taken part in an herbicide spraying program along railroad tracks, death caused by tumors had occurred at four times the rate normally to be expected.

In February 1979, the federal Environmental Protection Agency (EPA) suspended the use of herbicides containing 2,4,5-T in forests and pastures, near homes and recreation areas, and along roads and railway tracks. The compound is still used on rice fields and cattle ranges.

BARBED WIRE

During the weeks following the Seveso accident, animals continued to die and many people sickened. Examination of the dead animals showed enormously swollen, disintegrating livers and kidneys. Adults and children were stricken with some 200 cases of chloracne, and doctors found many cases of liver enlargement.

When researchers and government officials realized how deadly a poison had been spread over the area, they decided to close off the section most seriously affected. The highest number of animal deaths had occurred right in the path of the cone-shaped cloud. This area—267 acres (108 hectares) directly south of the factory—was designated as Zone A. It was cleared of all its 739 inhabitants and declared out of bounds to everyone except specially clothed salvage crews. At its borders, Zone B was made available for limited access. And all around, a further region was declared a Zone of Respect.

Barbed wire barriers were strung around Zone A, with Italian troops clad in protective suits to guard them. For Angela and Paolo Venturi, it meant saying good-bye to their beloved house and garden for many months, probably for years. Without any of their furnishings, toys, or clothing, the Venturis were evacuated from danger Zone A and brought to live in a hotel near Milan. Later, they moved into a small apartment there. Among the hundreds of other evacuees who were given a series of medical examinations, they were lucky enough to show relatively low dioxin contamination. They had been careful not to eat fruit and vegetables from their garden. Only poor Yip, suffering from diarrhea and in evident pain, had had to be left behind with a veterinarian. He did not survive.

Bordering the highway that runs from Milan to the northern lakes of Italy, a plastic fence was erected to shield motorists from the most heavily contaminated part of Seveso. Signs along the grim, yellow barrier read "Contaminated Zone." Even two years later, drivers were still warned to close all vents and windows and to drive on slowly without stopping, so as not to stir up dioxin-contaminated dust.

DEAD LEAVES AND CARCASSES

Cleaning up after a pollution accident is dangerous and expensive. The Seveso explosion was the first of its kind. Around the world, only a few, far more limited, dioxin accidents had occurred. Experts called in to give advice on restoring order made many impractical suggestions. These included such ideas as removing a deep layer of earth and spraying everything with a layer of plastic; washing everything with white soap; spraying the entire community with olive oil; and burning everything to the ground with a flame thrower. This last suggestion horrified scientists who realized that, far from destroying the toxins, such superficial burning would only spread them for miles through the air.

Officials of the ICMESA company soon realized that the factory building could not be touched for some time. Throughout Zone A, workers in white protective masks and suits picked up dead leaves and dead animals with gloved hands, and stuffed them into plastic bags. The soil itself turned out to be contaminated in some spots to a depth of 12 inches (30.48 cm). The workers buried as many of the plastic bags as possible in deep trenches. But thousands of other bags, bursting with decayed and contaminated matter remain piled up in storehouses, awaiting further action.

Dioxin is thought to decompose gradually under the action of sunlight. Otherwise there seems to be no way of ridding ourselves of this devilish substance. Free dioxins are destroyed by incineration at about 800 degrees C (1,475 degrees F). But dioxins bound to any sort of particulate matter can pass through incinerators operating at temperatures as high as about 1150 degrees C (2,100 degrees F) with no change in concentration.

For two years, workers in Zones A and B cut down trees, took down roofs of houses, broke furniture, vacuumed and washed walls of homes and schools with detergents and olive oil, and buried the wastes. Then, a few families were permitted to move back into their houses.

In fact, though, the cleaning has not been highly effective. Dioxin particles have been turning up in a far wider area than the zone originally contaminated. For one thing, hundreds of dead animals, sent to laboratories for autopsies and chemical investigation, ended up in the waste disposal incinerators of Milan. The temperature in these incinerators is just high enough to send minute dioxin-laden particles into the air through the chimneys.

Then, too, contaminated dust was picked up by wind and blown further away, while heavy autumn floods washed contaminated soil downriver. Cars driving through the region picked up dioxin particles in spite of all precautions, and rescue workers, with all their care, still could not avoid carrying the substance back and forth on their shoe soles.

One feared result has not occurred. The water of the Lombardy region has not become heavily contaminated with dioxin. The reason, apparently, is that the subsoil under the Seveso region consists of heavy clay. Large deposits of the toxin seem to have become lodged in cracks and crevices, and there, for the time being, they remain.

VENGEANCE:
A SENSELESS MURDER

Four years after the explosion at Seveso, a group of people riding together in one car ambushed, shot, and killed the thirty-nine-year-old chief engineer of the ICMESA factory. It is doubtful that the chief engineer was directly responsible for the accident. Yet, a sense of injustice and the craving for revenge among the population of the area were strong enough to derange a few individuals to the point of committing senseless murder. Though thousands of lives were disrupted, the Swiss parent company that owns the ICMESA plant has yet to be brought to court, and scores of lawsuits are still pending.

CHAPTER III
HOW HAZARDOUS MATERIALS AFFECT THE BODY

WHAT IS HARMFUL?

Most of the chemicals we use in our everyday lives pose no threat to our health and safety. But even the most "harmless" material can be dangerous under certain conditions. Underwater divers, for example, are often surprised to learn that one of the many hazards they face is the breathing of oxygen under high pressure. Oxygen at pressures that greatly exceed normal atmospheric pressure can be toxic.

The dangers posed by pollutants are more obvious. These undesirable substances are known to cause injury, illness, and perhaps death. Yet even here, the damage caused by any specific material will depend on many factors. The human body is a very complicated and delicately balanced system. Each of its cells is constantly producing, by means of thousands of chemical reactions, the substances needed for its growth and protection. When toxic material is absorbed, it can disrupt these natural chemical processes and damage both the cells and the organs that contain them.

The damage sustained by the body will depend not only on the concentration of the pollutant but also on the rate of absorption and on the length of exposure. Exposure to a hazardous substance, for example, can be acute (delivered all at once) or chronic (repeated over a prolonged period of time.) To further complicate matters, people have different sensitivities to toxic materials. Often, the presence of two toxic substances working together produces a synergistic effect. That is, the total effect is greater than that produced by equivalent concentrations of each substance given alone.

CHEMICAL TRACES

The chemistry of the cell can be affected by astonishingly small amounts of foreign substances. Often, toxic substances are present in such small trace amounts that special ways of describing them are needed.

It is hard to imagine a unit that expresses the presence of 1 ounce (28.35 g) of salt in 62,500 pounds (28,400 kg) of sugar. Yet this small ratio of salt to sugar, one part salt to one million parts sugar, written as 1 ppm (that is, part per million), is the standard way of expressing the concentration of pollutants in the environment. Negligible as they may appear, pollutant concentrations of this size can be dangerous. One ppm in water of the common disinfectant carbolic acid, for example, can be lethal to some fish. As little as one thousandth of a ppm of hydrogen fluoride gas in the atmosphere can damage peach trees.

Modern analytical instruments, such as the mass spectrometer, are even capable of detecting traces of substances in concentrations as small as 1 part per billion. In many environmental laboratories, these ultrasensitive instruments, along with high-speed computers, are replacing the traditional test tubes of chemical analysis. With a mass spectrometer, trace contaminants have been found whose presence was never suspected before.

FOOD CHAINS

Big fish eat little fish, as we all know. They are, in turn, eaten by even bigger fish, or else by humans. This series of events in which organisms are absorbed up the ladder, as it were, is called a food chain.

Most Americans are lucky enough to eat high on the food

chain. This may not be an unmixed blessing, though. Some pollutants remain stored in the organism that absorbs them, and as they are swallowed by one eater after another, the concentrations of these pollutants actually increase as they move up the food chain.

Gulls feeding in Lake Michigan, for example, have extremely high concentrations of DDT in their tissues. DDT is not soluble in water, but it is soluble in fat. The insecticide cannot be detoxified once it enters a live organism. It cannot be broken down by the digestive system and will, therefore, simply accumulate in the fatty tissues. A worm might have a small quantity of DDT in its tissue, but a fish that eats many worms can accumulate increasing amounts every time it eats. The study of one food chain in Lake Michigan found 0.014 ppm in the mud sediment at the bottom of the lake, 3 to 6 ppm in various fish, and over 2,400 ppm in fish-eating gulls.

DECOMPOSITION

The longer we are in contact with toxic pollutants, the greater the danger they pose. Most naturally occurring chemicals are biodegradable. This means that they are quickly broken down by some form of life, usually by bacteria. Such biological transformations have evolved over millions of years and are part of the natural cycle of living material.

Many of the new materials synthesized by chemists in recent years, however, are not part of this cycle. They decompose very slowly, depending on chemical reactions that might take place in soil, or water, or in the presence of sunlight. Chlorinated hydrocarbons, for example, the group of chemical compounds that are active as insecticides and herbicides, require some ten to fifteen years to decompose to half their potency in soil. Certain pollutants, such as lead, never change. They remain dangerous forever.

HOW TOXIC IS IT?

The toxicity of many substances that are suspected of being harmful is usually evaluated by means of a series of tests on animals. The results are then applied to human beings. Great care must be used in evaluating these results since different species may react quite differently to the same toxic substance.

The animals most commonly used for these tests are rats. The animals are fed, or made to inhale, the toxic substance under study, and the lethal dose is measured. These lethal doses are usually expressed as LD_{50}, the amount of the substance that is fatal to 50 percent of the experimental group. Since larger animals will necessarily require more dosage than smaller ones, the LD_{50} is now expressed in terms of concentration per animal body weight. Thus the LD_{50} for aspirin was established as 1,500 mg/kg for a group of rats. Sodium cyanide, on the other hand, an extremely toxic substance, has an LD_{50} of only 6.4 mg/kg.

Other tests have been devised by the World Health Organization and other laboratories for specific effects, such as carcinogenesis. Conclusions drawn from these experiments have led to some controversy about their validity, since large doses in a short period of time are often given to animals. Opponents of restrictive regulations have ridiculed these tests and adopted the slogan "everything causes cancer." It is true that care must be taken in interpreting the results, since, in reality, small doses are usually absorbed over a long period of time. Nevertheless, the EPA released statistics in 1979 that stated that only 7 percent of the 7,000 compounds studied by means of high-dose animal tests have displayed carcinogenic characteristics.

CHROMOSOME DAMAGE

Nothing seems more magical than the ability of the cells in our body to make exact replicas of themselves. The information needed to make these copies is carried by chromosomes in the form of thousands of genetic particles called genes.

The chromosomes are tiny threadlike bodies found in the nucleus of every cell in the human system. The word "chromosome" is derived from the Greek words "chroma," for color, and "soma," for body, because chromosomes can be colored by certain stains that permit biologists to study them. Human beings have twenty-three pairs of chromosomes in each cell, and each pair can be identified by shape and size.

Damage to chromosomes is an important test of whether people have been exposed to toxic chemicals or dangerous radiation. The damage usually results in breaking the chromosome strand into fragments. Occasionally, some chromosome material may be missing or new material added.

The damage is hard to interpret, however, since everyone usually has some chromosome damage caused by the quite ordinary events of our everyday life. Sunlight, common colds, flu, dental X-rays, can all damage chromosomes.

Usually, a cell with damaged chromosomes will die. Sometimes, though, cells can even repair the broken strands. In recent years, scientists believe they have discovered a correlation between physical abnormalities in humans and the number of damaged chromosomes produced by toxic material. Cancer, birth defects, and miscarriages have all been related to chromosome fragments. The strongest evidence comes from the survivors of the atomic bomb in Hiroshima. Recent studies have focused on some of the former residents of Love Canal, a dumping site near Buffalo, New York, which will be discussed later on in this book. The findings of these tests are unclear, however, and indicate the need for further research.

DNA AND CANCER

The overall rate of cancer has been increasing in our society. There is now a general consensus that the great majority of cancers are due to environmental factors. Data on occupational carcinogenesis have been accumulated since the eighteenth century. There are well documented examples of bladder cancer in the aniline dye and rubber industry, lung cancer in uranium miners and nitrogen mustard gas workers, nasal sinus cancer in woodworkers, and a host of others.

In trying to understand how such a variety of substances can cause cancer, scientists are investigating DNA, the body's genetic material. DNA (deoxyribonucleic acid) controls the manufacture of proteins in each cell in the body.

The structure of DNA is in the form of a double helix, resembling a twisted ladder. Each "rung" of the ladder contains complex pairs of molecules called nucleotide bases. The order of these base pairs up the ladder carries the information that controls the protein manufacture. Cancer causing substances bind to these rungs and distort the form of the helix. Scientists believe that this distortion leads to genetic errors in replication that can induce cancerous cells. The body contains enzymes that have the ability to recognize these errors and even to remove them. Many toxic substances are known to damage or impair the efficiency of these enzymes.

It has also recently become apparent that many cancer producing substances are inactive in their natural form and start the cancer process only after they have been converted to a highly active form in the body. Many of these active forms are chemical changes that permit the body to excrete them more easily. It seems paradoxical that the activation of many carcinogenic substances is part of the body's natural defense system.

ROUTES OF HUMAN EXPOSURE
Hazardous materials can enter the body in at least three important ways: inhalation, skin contact, and ingestion. It is possible, of course, for human exposure to occur through more than one route. Children living in dilapidated housing are often exposed to lead poisoning by both eating peeled paint and inhaling lead particles from automobile exhaust. Exposure to insecticides can take place through all three routes at the same time. It is interesting to note that in a recent government publication listing 579 hazardous materials, 138 were indicated as showing significant absorption through the skin, the entry route least often considered.

RESPIRATORY SYSTEM
The respiratory system is the most potentially hazardous route by which toxic materials can enter the body, since

gases are almost immediately absorbed into the blood-stream following inhalation.

Basically, the respiratory tract is a system of tubes connecting the outside air with blood vessels in the lung. The air starts downward through the trachea, or windpipe. The trachea divides into two bronchial tubes, each of which enters a lung. Within the lung, each bronchus divides again into a treelike arrangement of smaller and smaller bronchi. At the end of the slenderest bronchi are some 400 million air sacs called alveoli. These air sacs are surrounded by capillaries so thin that the blood cells must pass through in single file. It is through the membranes of the alveoli that oxygen passes into the blood and that carbon dioxide is removed. The total surface area of alveoli is almost as large as a tennis court.

The respiratory system has several defense mechanisms to guard against harmful substances. The upper airways are lined with a sticky mucous membrane that catches small particles. Tiny hairs called cilia, that are in continuous wave-like motion, then sweep the trapped particles out so that they can be eliminated by swallowing or expectoration.

The spongy tissue composing the alveoli is particularly sensitive to air pollutants. When attacked by irritants, the tissue gradually increases what is called its leakage rate, causing more and more fluid to leave the blood and fill the air sacs. This oversecretion of fluid is called edema, and it reduces the lung space available for air. A weakening of the heart may follow as the heart strains harder and harder to compensate for the reduced flow of oxygen.

If contaminants stay too long in the respiratory tract, the result can be emphysema (taken from the Greek word for swelling). Scarring of the alveoli causes their delicate walls to burst. The tearing of the air-sac wall destroys the capillaries through which blood would ordinarily receive oxygen, and gradually a condition of oxygen starvation develops.

CHEMICAL ASPHYXIANT

Oxygen starvation, or asphyxia, can also be induced by pollutants that interfere with the oxygen carriers in the blood. Carbon monoxide is an example of a chemical asphyxiant, that is, a gas that prevents the body from receiving an adequate supply of oxygen. The common symptoms of carbon monoxide poisoning are headache, nausea, and difficulty in breathing. Since it is not possible to see or to smell the gas, these symptoms are usually the first warning that carbon monoxide is present.

Oxygen is normally transported to the body tissues by the hemoglobin in the red blood cells. The hemoglobin loosely binds with the oxygen received from the lungs to form a compound called oxyhemoglobin. The blood then flows into the body tissues where the oxygen is released. Hemoglobin, however, has a much greater chemical affinity for carbon monoxide than for oxygen. Given a choice between carbon monoxide and oxygen, that is, it will choose to combine with carbon monoxide. Any hemoglobin molecule carrying carbon monoxide will not be available for carrying oxygen, so that the oxygen reaching the tissues is drastically reduced.

PHOTOCHEMICAL OXIDANTS

Nitrogen dioxide is an acrid, reddish gas that is formed in large quantities by the burning of oil and coal in industrial and power plants. Automobile emissions, from both gasoline and diesel engines, also contribute a large share of this noxious substance.

Exposure to nitrogen dioxide has been known to result in serious illness and even death. The exposure to as little as 0.06 ppm over a long period of time has been related to an increase in respiratory diseases in humans. Exposure of 15 ppm for even short periods of time has produced changes in lung tissue similar to those occurring in emphysema. Concentrations of 100 ppm can be deadly.

The most important problem with nitrogen dioxide, however, occurs when the gas is exposed to sunlight. The sunlight stimulates chemical reactions which produce a whole new series of irritants known as oxidants. These photochemical reactions are possible with nitrogen dioxide because its reddish color permits it to absorb energy from the sun.

Chief among the oxidants is ozone, a gas that is also produced near high voltage transmission lines. Recently, another group of oxidants, the peroxyacyl nitrates (PAN compounds), has been found to be important also. The presence of these oxidants distinguishes the notorious Los Angeles smog (called photochemical smog) from the more classical "London fog" which contains sulphur compounds from the burning of coal.

OZONE
Most materials deteriorate with time because of changes in their structure due to oxidation. This chemical change usually involves the addition of oxygen to the molecules that make up the material. The presence of ozone greatly accelerates the rate at which these reactions occur. Ozone, as well as other photochemical oxidants, is known to injure plants and vegetables and cause severe eye, nose, and throat irritation. Smog irritation is detectable at ozone levels as low as 0.15 ppm. Levels of 1 ppm have been measured in Los Angeles.

Recent studies have shown that there are increased numbers of bacteria in lung tissue that has been exposed to ozone. This seems to be due to the oxidation induced by ozone of an antibacterial enzyme contained in lung cells. Another important finding is that ozone affects macrophage cells. These cells have the ability to ingest foreign particles including bacteria, entering the lung. Ozone has also been shown to reduce, by as much as 70 percent, the activity of certain enzymes that attack and detoxify carcinogens found in cigarette smoke and smoke from charcoal-broiled meats.

AIRBORNE DUST
Pollutants can also enter the lung in the form of particles. Hippocrates, as far back as 400 B.C., recognized and described some of the classic symptoms of lung disease in miners digging for metals.

The word "pneumoconiosis" is derived from two words: "pneumo," meaning lung, and "conis," meaning dust.

It is used to describe a condition of the lung that is also known as fibrosis. Here, inhaled dust causes the lung tissue to harden and form fibers that resemble scar tissue. The chief materials causing pneumoconiosis are coal dust, asbestos, and silicates such as quartz. "Silicosis" and "asbestosis" are other names given to this condition. The disease is irreversible and leads to improper and insufficient oxygen transfer in the lungs. Asbestos dust is also responsible for lung cancer and a fatal malignant disease called mesothelioma. This disease occurs some twenty-five to forty years after the initial exposure.

METALS

Most of us are aware that arsenic is poisonous. It is more difficult to think of the lead in a fishing weight or the chromium plating on a serving tray as harmful. All three of these metals, though, are toxic when taken into the body. They are examples of a class of potentially hazardous materials called heavy metals. Included in this group are mercury, cadmium, and beryllium, among some thirty others of toxicological interest. These metals are called heavy, because they are extremely dense.

All metals are toxic if given in sufficient doses. Strangely enough, though, in small amounts some metals are essential to life, since they are biologically important components of blood cells, enzymes, and vitamins.

Brain cells and the nervous system are particularly sensitive to heavy-metal poisoning. The symptoms of mercury poisoning, now called "Minamata Disease," which include tremors, lack of muscular coordination, and paralysis, are largely those of improper neurological functioning. Lead, one of the oldest known toxic metals, has recently been suspected of damaging the brain development of millions of children through chronic exposure to gasoline, plumbing, tobacco smoke, canning, and industrial emissions. Lead poisoning is probably the major neuro-toxic disease in this country.

PASSAGE THROUGH THE BODY

After being absorbed, the toxic material enters the blood stream and travels through the circulatory system. As toxicants travel through the body they ultimately contact all the organs. Many show a preference for the cells of a particular organ, while others injure all the cells they contact. Mercury and lead, for example, after being inhaled, can damage the central nervous system and the kidneys. Benzene attacks the blood-forming organs, and carbon tetrachloride the liver.

Fortunately, the body possesses natural mechanisms for converting harmful chemicals into harmless ones or into substances that are easily excreted. Many ingested pollutants, for example, are inactivated by the digestive process. There are also substances that pass through the entire gastrointestinal tract unchanged without causing any adverse effect, while still others may damage the entire mucosal lining of the stomach and intestines.

Certain tissues of the body act like a storage depot for toxic materials. Interestingly, the toxicant does no harm while being stored. Gradually, it is released through various metabolic processes, and as it re-enters the mainstream of the body it can cause injury. Fatty tissues store DDT, for example, while bone tissues act as a reservoir for lead and tetracycline.

RADIOACTIVITY
AND ITS EFFECTS

We live in a sea of radiation. Nuclear reactors and their waste products are only a relatively minor source of radiation. Radiation reaches us from outer space, and our very bodies contain radioactive isotopes, such as potassium-40 and carbon-14.

Radiation can damage the human body because it has the ability to disrupt physically the atoms and molecules that make up basic cells. When radiant energy is absorbed, it strips electrons from atoms along its path. This process is called ionization. The injury to the cell is generally proportional to the amount of ionization produced in the cell. Because of its ionizing power, the radiation can produce new highly reactive chemicals within the cell. These chemicals "poison" the cell by attacking vital enzymes and other metabolic agents. The effects on the body as a whole, however, vary considerably and depend on the type of radiation received as well as the type of cell injured or destroyed. Radiation may also damage chromosomes and cause mutation of genes that will be inherited by future generations.

When radioactive isotopes are ingested, the organs affected vary with the radioisotope. Uranium and plutonium affect the bone, sulfur-35 the testes, and iodine-131 the thyroid gland. Both internal and external exposure to radiation can cause skin cancer, bone cancer, leukemia, eye cataracts, and premature aging.

The most common units for measuring radiation and its effects are the Roentgen (R) and the Roentgen Equivalent Man (REM). They both express the amount of energy deposited in the form of ionization in exposed material. The REM, which is a newer unit, contains more information since it also estimates the biological effect of various types of radiation.

Guidelines for maximum permissible doses are usually expressed in millirem (one thousandth of a REM). The allowable dose for pregnant women and persons under the age of eighteen, for example, is 10 millirem. An exposure of 75,000 millirem will begin to induce some of the common symptoms of radiation sickness, such as skin reddening (erythema) and a drop in white blood cell count. An exposure of 450,000 millirem will usually be lethal to 50 percent of the population exposed.

HALF-LIFE
Radioactive elements behave as if they contained an internal clock. Their concentration is constantly decreasing at a fixed rate which never changes. The element does not disappear but changes itself into a new element.

Every radioactive element has its own characteristic rate of breakdown. The rate is most conveniently expressed in terms of half-lives. The half-life specifies the time required for half the atoms of a radioactive element to disintegrate. Radioactive elements have a wide range of half-lives, and no two of them are the same. Uranium-238, the major component of natural uranium, for example, has an extremely long half-life of 4.5 billion years. If we started out with 2 pounds (0.91 kg) of this uranium, after 4.5 billion years we would still have 1 pound (0.45 kg) left. Other radioactive elements have much shorter half-lives. Iodine-131, with a half-life of 8.1 days, and krypton-85, with a half-life of 10.7 years, are examples of important radioactive contaminants formed in nuclear reactors.

Since the concentration of the radioactive element decreases by half during each half-life, periods of time corresponding to 5 or 10 half-lives will produce dramatic drops in concentration. At the end of 10 half-lives, for example, only one thousandth the original concentration remains.

CHAPTER IV
ONE TENTH
OF ONE PERCENT:
POLLUTANTS
IN AIR

The Grand Canyon is one of the world's most impressive sights. Nowadays, though, it is often filled with haze. This is due to emissions from a power plant many miles away. At times, visibility becomes less than fifteen miles, so that visitors can't even see across the canyon to the opposite rim.

Air pollution is an age-old problem. First of all, there are nature's own pollutants, composed of flying dry earth particles, yeast, pollens, molds, and bacteria. For many centuries, smoke from burning coal was the most harmful source of air pollution. It not only caused a wide range of ailments but also coated city buildings in deepest black. In the early 1900s, motor vehicles began spewing out carbon monoxide which now accounts for 52 percent of our total tonnage of airborne pollutants. Finally, since World War II, synthetic chemistry has been emitting a new mixture of compounds into the breathing space around us.

It may surprise you that, actually, the pollutants suspended in the air we breathe at any given time make up only ⅔ of 1/10 of 1 percent of the total air. As for moisture, even on the most humid days the air can hold little more than 1 percent of water. All the same, the amount of foreign matter in the air over the United States each year reaches up to 200 million metric tons, or about one ton per person.

The stuff we inhale, then, is a kind of weak broth of chemicals and water vapor. The ingredients react with one another or come under the influence of the sun's energy, so that the broth undergoes constant changes. It heats up and cools down, rises and falls, and is moved by winds.

Studies have shown that, in general, automobiles and trucks are the major contributors to air pollution, accounting for 60 percent of total tons emitted. Industry takes the next largest share of the responsibility with a contribution of 18 percent. Electric power generating plants contribute 13 percent. Space heating and garbage disposal contribute 6 and 3 percent, respectively.

Polluted air is also laden with a variety of small particles. On a windy day we may find one lodged in our eye or feel it grit between our teeth. This particulate matter escapes from many different manufacturing processes. It also comes from burning fuels, garbage incineration, and accidental fires. Particulate matter, suspended all around us, absorbs light, neutralizes colors, makes dark objects look yellowish rather than bluish, and reduces visibility into the distance.

Particulate matter may contain microscopic chemical droplets and minute metal fragments. The larger particles appear as unsightly dirt and grime and are damaging to plants and painted walls. The smaller particles, though, are more harmful than those we can see lying on our window sills, because we inhale them with the air we breathe. They enter our lungs and possibly our blood stream.

GASES

Combustion, the process of burning, produces many different gases, depending on the temperature and type of fuel consumed. Sulfur dioxide, carbon monoxide, hydrocarbons, and nitrogen dioxide are all combustion gases.

Sulfur dioxide comes from the burning of sulfurous coal and oil. The resulting fumes cause asthma, bronchitis, and other respiratory ailments.

35]

Carbon monoxide is emitted by automobiles, trucks, and buses. It results from incomplete combustion. More than 87 million tons of carbon monoxide are released into the air each year. That makes it America's most copious pollutant. It is a colorless and odorless gas which can cause death. Concentrated carbon monoxide in crowded city streets often causes faintness, headaches, and even heart attacks. When carbon monoxide is given a chance to disperse, it gradually becomes absorbed and degraded in nature. Recent research indicates that large quantities of carbon monoxide in the atmosphere are removed by soils, probably through the activity of microorganisms.

Hydrocarbons are emitted by the vapors of burning gasoline, paints, solvents, and dry cleaning compounds. Inhaled in high concentrations, such as might occur in an enclosed space, they induce drowsiness and headaches, fainting, and eventually liver damage and other severe effects on health.

In the atmosphere, hydrocarbons are chiefly of concern because they react under sunlight with other compounds, lose their invisibility, and turn into smog.

Nitrogen dioxide, finally, is produced in manufacturing when temperature is so high that the nitrogen, always present in air, also begins to burn. This is a gas which attacks the lungs and respiratory system.

SMOG

It is early May and the baseball season has been off to a good start. But on the field behind the high school, the play-

One of the worst air pollution episodes in modern times occurred in London in 1962. It is believed that the smog, over a period of days, was responsible for the deaths of almost 4,000 people.

ers can't seem to get moving. The temperature is in the mid-eighties, and for two days this greenbelt suburb has been wrapped in yellow haze. The smog that settled in after a week of clear crisp weather is making everyone sluggish and irritable. There are no factory chimneys near. Where could this smog have come from?

Smog is the popular name for many combinations of photochemical oxidant compounds in the air. Oxidants are formed when other pollutants, sometimes called precursors, combine and react with one another under the influence of sunlight. Precursor compounds suspended in air do not always react with each other immediately. In some cases a slow reaction takes place and is further developed by the sun. As air masses stagnate over industrial areas and highways, new compounds are constantly added to the chemical broth. Air masses may move for hundreds of miles, absorbing new pollutants as they travel along.

INVERSION LAYERS

The hazy air stagnating over the baseball field may have been brought there after being trapped in an "inversion layer." Warm air is lighter than cold air and ordinarily tends to rise. At times, though, warm air trying to rise is trapped under a layer of cold air trying to sink. Lying for days in this inverted position over an industrial area, the warm air will become saturated with different pollutant gases and particulates. Under the influence of sunlight, these will begin to simmer like soup in a covered pot. Then, temperature changes bring winds that push or draw the trapped layer many miles aloft. Freed now, it may move far from the original source and then sink once more toward the ground.

The oxidant that makes athletes sluggish and even prevents children from playing with their usual energy is ozone. It is not only the most abundant of the oxidant compounds but also the one that presents the most serious health hazard.

Ozone concentrations of .15 ppm and upward tend to trigger asthma attacks and aggravate heart disease. Ozone weakens and destroys red blood cells, so that it endangers sufferers from anemia.

AIRBORNE CARCINOGENS

Among the numberless substances that find their way into our air, some forty compounds suspected of causing cancer were placed under intensive study by the Environmental Protection Agency (EPA) in the late 1970s. Such known carcinogens as asbestos, benzene, beryllium, mercury, and vinyl chloride are already being monitored under new emission standards. Because offending factories have been forced to install air filters and other purifying devices, the EPA has found that the new standards have also reduced the level of a number of other toxic metals in air, such as vanadium, manganese, and nickel.

Quite recently, researchers in the United States and in several European countries have found dioxins in the ash of municipal incinerators. The amounts are small, but the presence in the air of this highly toxic substance may be causing considerable harm. Until now, the source of this dioxin is a mystery, since municipal incinerators burn mostly household trash and only a minor portion of industrial refuse.

LEAD

In addition to all these pollutants, more than 16,000 metric tons of lead are mixed into our air every year. Some of this amount is directly due to industry, but most of it is emitted by trucks and passenger cars. The world's lead production has been rising by leaps and bounds in the past five thousand years. In Roman times some 80,000 tons of it were produced each year; today we produce about three million tons of lead annually. This means that over the centuries, lead from industries has entered our air, water, soil, and food. People living in the twentieth century ingest far more lead than those who lived thousands of years ago. Lead in high concentrations is poisonous to the body, damaging the kidneys and the brain. In 1978, the EPA issued its first standards for limiting lead releases into the air and ordered nationwide compliance within nine months. Complete success of this effort, though, has been held up by legal suits in the courts.

ACID RAIN

The Adirondacks of northern New York State are a deeply forested mountain range dotted with lakes. Gradually, during the last five decades, more than half the lakes lying above 2,000 feet (610 m) have lost their fish. Now the waters that were once so clear are rapidly filling with mosses, algae, and fungi.

Tall smoke stacks of coal-fired factories and power plants generate tons of sulfuric acid and nitric acid to be carried aloft and driven on by winds. Gasoline and diesel-burning engines contribute their share of corrosive pollutants. Eventually, these acids are dissolved in rain or in the crystals of snow, and so they return to earth. In parts of the world where these acids still come to the soil and water in rather small quantities, they are gradually neutralized. In the northeastern United States, though, factories from both sides of the Canadian border have started to overwhelm forested areas, and especially those which are in the mountains and receive a greater share of rain and snow than flatlands. Now there is evidence of acidity spreading to the South and West. Luckily, western soil tends to be so strongly alkaline that it neutralizes acid rain very quickly.

Acid rain destroys the protective coating of plant tissues, removes nutrients from foliage, and causes scars and deformities in the leaves. Once the acid water reaches the ground it hastens the leaching out, or removal, of calcium, magnesium, potassium, and sodium—all important nutrients for plant life. Acid moisture inhibits nitrogen fixing bacteria and increases root absorption of certain harmful metals. It attacks the trees from above and also causes them to become starved and poisoned at the roots.

Fish have difficulty reproducing and surviving in acid water and tend gradually to die out over a number of decades.

Sometimes, though, a sudden acid-laden snowfall can kill thousands of fish in a day by acid shock.

Acid rain destroys the metal of auto bodies and the paint on houses. It corrodes public statues and sculptures, marble steps, and stone buildings. It threatens to destroy some magnificent historic and artistic monuments of Europe. Chiefly, however, scientists studying acid rain under laboratory conditions are concerned about the future of our timberland, our fruit and vegetable crops, and even our maple sugar.

Acid rain has recently become more and more acidic. The phenomenon is all the more deplorable since it is entirely avoidable. Fossil-fueled factories can equip their chimneys with scrubbers that eliminate acid precipitation as well as other small particles in coal smoke. Government experts estimate that scrubbers add no more than 15 percent to the cost of operating coal-fired plants.

CHAPTER V
HAZMAT: STORING AND SHIPPING HAZARDOUS MATERIALS

On an April morning in 1974 some of the eleven thousand inhabitants of a housing project in Chicago found their windows blanketed by a thick fog. At the same time, a choking odor of gas drove many of them out into the street. Their eyes filled with tears, their throats burned. Some had such difficulty breathing that they lost consciousness. Others tried to help themselves by holding wet towels over their mouths and noses. They waited in silent huddles for police vans to move them to a school building a few miles away. But when they filed into the school the wind shifted the fumes in their direction, as if to pursue them. By the end of the day, three hundred children and adults had been hospitalized.

A few blocks away, in a freight yard by the railroad, a storage tank had sprung a leak during the night. The tank held 750,000 gallons (2.85 million l) of silicon tetrachloride. As the corrosive chemical oozed through a crack at the rate of 100 gallons (380 l) a minute, it combined with water in the air and formed hydrogen chloride. This extremely irritating substance burns the skin and eyes, and, if inhaled, it may permanently damage the lungs and other organs.

Emergency crews vainly tried to stop the leak. Because

hydrogen chloride can be explosive, fire fighters, called to the scene, attempted to douse the tank with water. This was not a good idea because the spray combined with the leaking chemical to produce a concentrated mist of hydrochloric acid, extremely corrosive to human skin and mucous membranes.

Workmen in gas masks next attempted to bury the leaking crack in concrete. The crack became lost in the hardening cement mixture, but the toxic chemical continued to escape. Five days later, the leak was finally sealed. By that time, luckily for the people living in the housing project, the wind shifted to carry the fumes away over Lake Michigan.

Such accidents are everyday occurrences in the storage and transportation of hazardous material—HAZMAT, as it is called in the railroading trade. HAZMAT includes materials that are explosive, corrosive, flammable, or radioactive, as well as gases that are damaging or even lethal if they are inhaled.

DEATH ON RAILS

Four billion tons of hazardous materials are shipped across our nation each year. More than half of these shipments travel by rail. In spite of the gradual decline of passenger railroad travel in recent decades and the closing of many rail lines, it is still considered more economical to transport freight by train than by truck. Unfortunately, each year an increasing amount of hazardous freight has been traveling along the aging tracks of a more and more neglected railroad system. Many rail companies, claiming to be on the verge of bankruptcy, have lowered their standards for maintenance and supervision. As a result, accidents have been on the increase.

On a fairly typical date—January 14, 1980—as many as three different trains carrying hazardous material in three different states derailed. In Ohio, two thousand people fled their homes as overturned and damaged rail cars poured a stream of chemicals over their gardens and yards. In Arizona, twelve hundred inhabitants had to leave their houses when six cars derailed, two of them carrying highly explosive liquid propane gas. Finally, in Pennsylvania, still on the same date, a number of families had to be evacuated after derailment of a train carrying dangerous chemicals. Such events are so common that they do not make national headlines.

No lives were lost in these particular mishaps. But in 1978, twenty-two people were killed in just two accidents. In Tennessee a crew of fourteen railroad workers lost their lives when a car carrying liquid petroleum gas exploded. It had derailed two days earlier and seemed to be harmlessly at rest on its side when it suddenly erupted. In Florida, eight people died after inhaling chlorine fumes escaping from a derailed freight train 146 cars long.

Rescue crews rushing to the scene of an accident are often in great danger. In the Florida accident, a young volunteer fire fighter spotted a group of children approaching the wreck of a tank car leaking deadly epichlorohydrin gas. By running through the spill to warn them, he saved the children's lives but almost lost his own. He collapsed, unable to breathe. Although hospitalized for a long time, he has not made a full recovery but still suffers chest pains, shortness of breath, nausea, and headaches. He also faces the possibility that he may develop lung cancer.

Without loss of lives, railroad accidents that happen in unpopulated countrysides can still cause a great deal of devastation. There is a seven-acre cornfield in Ohio, for example, that has remained unused since 1978. In March of that year, some 20,000 gallons (76,000 l) of the cancer causing substance, ortho-toluidine, drenched the earth from an overturned train. To date, efforts to decontaminate the soil have not been successful.

A YELLOW-GREEN GAS

For most of us, chlorine is a common household product. We are used to chlorine compounds in our laundry bleach, our water supply, and our swimming pools. One of the most widely used chemicals today, liquid chlorine in concentrated

Deadly gas rises from cars of a freight train
that derailed in Youngstown, Florida, in 1978.
The gas killed 6 and injured 38 others.

form is also one of the deadliest. When liquid chlorine is allowed to escape from its pressurized tank, it mingles with air and expands into a yellow-green gas that has a sweetish odor. This gas can kill those who inhale it in less than a minute by actually corroding the lungs. In the same Florida accident that caused the collapse of a rescue worker, four of the victims were high school students killed in their car. The fumes had stalled the engine, and the young people died while trying to jump out and run. So corrosive is concentrated chlorine gas that it even disintegrated the coins in the victims' pockets.

RESCUE OPERATIONS

When a freight train jumps the tracks, national and regional response teams, health officers, fire fighters, and clean-up companies rush to the scene. Their first job is to find out what is in the overturned cars. If any substance is likely to explode, they must evacuate the people living in the area and wait until it seems safe to approach the wreck. Clad in gas masks, gloves, and heat-resistant protective clothing, rescue experts, aware of danger, walk toward the wreckage cautiously. They listen for hissing sounds which would betray leaking gases or escaping liquids under pressure. Workers at the scene must know how to neutralize various corrosive chemicals. Chlorine, for example, is neutralized with caustic soda, known to chemists as sodium hydroxide. Rescue workers are aware that they cannot douse chemical fires with water. Water tends to combine with certain compounds to form other toxic mixtures and to fill the air with a deadly mist. Instead of water, a thick blanket of sprayed foam is used to smother chemical fires. In some cases, fire fighters may need earth and sand to put the fire out. Sometimes, the fire cannot be put out at all but must be allowed to burn out.

When all danger of fire is past, heavy lifting and digging equipment is brought to the wreckage site. Salvage crews now begin the job of straightening out fallen rail cars, pumping remaining liquids from the wreck into sound new tanks, removing bent and broken tracks, and replacing them with new sections so that train traffic can continue. In restoring order, salvage experts must prevent spilled toxics from entering nearby bodies of water where they might kill fish and poison drinking water.

Frequently, too, several different kinds of hazardous cargo travel together on one train. The explosion of one type of cargo might set another cargo on fire and release the corrosive vapors of yet a third. No wonder one commentator compares a freight car wreck to a ticking time bomb!

HAVOC ON THE HIGHWAY
While an estimated 1,654 railroad cars were involved in spills of hazardous material during 1977, a far greater number of spills—14,270—took place on our country's highways.

Let us look at an accident that occurred on a country road in Ohio. A tank truck carrying some 600 gallons (2,280 l) of beer-can lacquer struck a passenger car, slid across the road, wrapped itself around a tree, and sprung a leak. The driver of the truck and three women in the car were killed by the collision.

The lacquer, used to give beer and soda cans their shiny finish, is a mixture of three materials implicated in causing cancer, birth defects, and organ damage. They are polyvinyl chloride, toluene, and ketone. Yet highway police arriving on the scene and forced to inhale the vapors of this brew pouring across the road had no way of knowing just what they were confronting. The truck's papers on which the cargo is supposed to be registered were in the crushed and flattened cab with the dead driver. It took two hours just to extricate the body. The road remained closed for the day, until the liquid oozing from the vehicle could be identified. Among the rescue workers, one was blinded, others were hospitalized. It is conceivable that they sustained permanent health damage.

Only the word Flammable, printed on the truck's side, indicated that it carried some sort of hazardous material. Although drivers are required to carry papers specifying the

A tank truck carrying liquid styrene overturned,
spilling the flammable substance over a
Connecticut highway. Fire fighters sprayed the area
with foam to prevent the possibility of fire.

contents of the tank, these often give only the company name for the product. This may be a name such as "Mix 99," which leaves one to guess the precise chemical composition. Besides, trucks carrying loads that are explosive, corrosive, or flammable, are required to carry warnings only if the load weighs over 1,000 pounds (450 kg). Regulations such as these undergo frequent changes as lawmakers attempt to improve safety. Added to the confusion are differences between federal, state, and local regulations.

One rule is well established, though. Truckers ferrying hazardous substances are required by law to avoid certain roads, especially those that lead through populous areas or through tunnels. But often, traffic is slow and drivers in a hurry have been known to take dangerous shortcuts. In fact, most of us, driving along the highway, hardly suspect what a deadly array of combustibles, explosives, corrosives, and compressed gases are hurtling along next to us.

BLEVE

A unique type of explosive accident, the BLEVE (it rhymes with "heavy"), involving tank cars carrying liquefied flammable gas has recently plagued the transportation system of this country. Observers often compare the awe-inspiring spectacle of a BLEVE to a nuclear explosion. The name BLEVE stands for Boiling Liquid Expanding Vapor Explosion. The violence of the detonation has devastated large areas and rocketed railroad container cars thousands of feet through the air. In one such accident, a town in Illinois was almost completely destroyed.

A BLEVE usually starts when some incident, such as a derailment, produces a fire that comes into contact with a tank of liquefied gas under pressure. Tanks of this kind always contain a safety device called a relief valve to relieve any excess pressure that might build up in the tank. As the tank begins to get hot, the pressure builds up and more and more of the gas escapes through the valve. Eventually, the liquid level falls below the point of contact of the flame on the container. With no liquid now in the immediate area of the heating to prevent excessive temperatures, tremendous strains are set up in the metal. Within a short period of time, the metal "fatigues" and the tank ruptures. The remaining liquid gas is released all at once and explodes with enormous violence.

Efforts have been made by government and railroad officials to train fire fighters and other safety personnel in methods to combat this kind of accident. Some progress in tank car design has also been made. Heavier head shields guard against punctures; new thermal shields provide better insulation; and improved coupling devices lessen the chance of disengagement. Still, the threat of a BLEVE is ever present in a society that depends more and more on gas as a source of its energy.

RADIOACTIVE MATERIALS

In midwinter of 1979, a 220 ton radioactive piece of a failed nuclear power plant traveled by barge from Tidewater, Virginia, to Richland, Washington. Scientists at the Hanford Federal installation in Washington State were planning to test the part to see why it had become corroded and had failed to function. The U.S. Department of Energy, which took charge of the shipment, contended that the operation would not add a significant amount of radiation to the route. At the same time, though, scientists at the Hanford laboratories admitted that the mammoth machine fragment, riding the water through the Panama Canal and up the Pacific Coast, would emit three times the amount of radiation permitted under the rules of the U.S. Department of Transportation.

Radioactive matter of one kind or another makes up about 20 percent of the hazardous material transported on our highways. In contrast to other dangerous substances, though, radioactive matter is kept closely guarded. It is also packed with great care, in special lead-lined containers constructed like bank vaults, and made to withstand a high degree of shock. In one accidental fall off a Tennessee cliff, a box containing radiation wastes remained without a dent or scratch.

Critics of nuclear power, though, point to several accidents involving radioactive shipments. A highway accident occurred in Colorado in 1976, when a truck carrying uranium concentrate swerved to avoid three horses and spilled a quarter of its 4,000 pound (1,800 kg) cargo.

Twice, in the early 1970s, the luggage compartments of passenger aircraft were contaminated by leaks in radioactive shipments that were carelessly packaged. The second incident was particularly serious because the shipment traveled on two trucks and two aircraft before the leak was detected. Unwittingly, airport employees, cargo handlers, and drivers received a radioactive dose. At last, on arrival at the receiving plant, the shipment set off the radiation alarm system when the truck backed towards the unloading platform. As a result of this latter accident the law now forbids carrying most types of radioactive cargo on passenger airplanes.

This questionable safety record also extends to transport and storage of low-level nuclear wastes. The wastes, in the form of used protective clothing, filters, and sludge, come from nuclear power plants, research laboratories, and hospitals administering anti-cancer radiation treatment and other types of nuclear medicine.

Until late in 1979, these low-level wastes were shipped without much ado to special sites in Nevada, South Carolina, and Washington, where they were buried in shallow trenches. But in October of that year, investigators of the disposal sites came upon leaking barrels, poor packaging, defective trucks, and inadequate protective fencing. Shippers had become careless. The governors of all three states temporarily closed the sites to any further waste disposal. Unfortunately, the overflow of hazardous wastes in nuclear medicine departments of hospitals became so serious that some of the sites were reopened a few weeks later. Since then, all shipments of radioactive material are closely monitored according to a new interstate agreement.

An even more serious problem is presented by the need to store so-called high level, long-lived nuclear waste products. Some of the elements in these wastes will remain active for hundreds of thousands—perhaps even for several millions—of years. Yet a panel of experts commissioned by the EPA in 1978 to investigate methods for depositing high-level wastes reported that none of the nuclear storage canisters they had inspected showed evidence of being able to survive much longer than a decade.

CHAPTER VI
WASTES THAT REFUSE TO DIE

Long ago, Number One Flower Street in Chester, Pennsylvania, may have been a garden cottage peeking from the shrubbery. By 1978, though, when the state's Environmental Resources Department fenced it off and plastered it with Keep Out signs, it had long been a blighted, ill-smelling dumping ground for chemical wastes.

The owner of the site was chiefly interested in collecting 55-gallon (209-l) steel drums for reprocessing. He later claimed he had no clear idea of what they contained. He was getting paid about a dollar a drum to stack them in his yard where he had previously set up a business in shredding old automobile tires.

The shipping company, on the other hand, which picked up the drums from a number of local chemical factories, received thousands of dollars to haul away what were known to be hazardous waste products. Ten thousand drums of various flammable and corrosive chemical wastes had piled up in the Flower Street yard when the mixture exploded in a gigantic fireball spewing pitch-black smoke. A bridge across the Delaware River had to be closed and forty-three fire fighters were hospitalized. Some of the fire fighters later found chemical corrosion holes in their tough protective clothing. For six hours it was feared that the flames would blow up the town's main gas tank, only a few yards away, as well as a neighboring storage yard containing liquefied natural gas under pressure.

The fire bankrupted the owner of Number One Flower Street and the property was sold at auction. The buyers, an electric power company, soon wished they had never made the purchase. Ownership made them liable for the costs of cleaning—approximately $3 million. A long legal battle loomed ahead. Meanwhile, the state was forced to build a fence around the scene of the explosion to keep children from investigating the charred debris.

Before the process of cleaning up can actually begin, the exact identity of the chemicals soaked into the ground must first be determined. But that is expensive detective work requiring the patient labor of chemical experts.

DUMPING HABITS

Until the early decades of this century, America had so much unoccupied land that communities simply dumped their trash and refuse on the outskirts of town. It was taken for granted that everything would eventually decompose into earth, out of which new grass and trees would grow. By midcentury, though, not only had the amount of refuse and industrial waste vastly increased, but much of it was of an entirely different quality. There now exist forms of plastics, chemical poisons, and radioactive substances that do not decompose into harmless earth but remain harmful for decades or even for hundreds and thousands of years. Today some of our wastes do not die, they just accumulate.

There are now 30,000 dump sites nationwide for the disposal of hazardous wastes. Most of these do not meet appropriate safety standards. In a survey begun in 1980, the EPA found that among the first 645 sites investigated, 100 pose a serious danger to some 600,000 people. Environmentalists estimate that over 200 million pounds (90 million kg)

Two men wearing protective suits handle damaged drums of arsenic that had been left on a New Orleans wharf.

of hazardous wastes are improperly disposed of every day. This figure represents about 90 percent of all hazardous wastes generated.

The major producers of hazardous wastes are metal refining and metal plating factories. Manufacturers of chemicals run a close second. Textile producers, petroleum refiners, and rubber and plastics manufacturers contribute a sizable share. All other industries combined produce only a small percentage of the total.

WHY WASTES ARE WASTED

It needs to be explained why chemical wastes are, indeed, wasted. For example, a solvent might contain 1 or 2 percent of a pesticide after a production run. The solvent cannot be reused in the next production run because the residue would cause equipment to break down or gum up. It is also possible that the manufacturing process would cause the residue to convert into some other undesirable substance. This would make the final product unsaleable. Why not purify it, you may ask? Most often, the reason is expense. It is actually cheaper to buy fresh, pure solvent than to purify the old solvent.

TOXIC PARK LAND

The newness of the toxic waste disposal problem has caught many communities entirely unprepared. On an island in the Ohio River near Pittsburgh, for example, government agencies spent $2 million developing a delightful recreation area. The land, donated by a local coke and chemical manufacturing corporation, had long been used as a disposal site for wastes of all kinds. But by 1979, walking trails, picnic areas, a marina, and a swimming pool were almost ready for opening to the public. Then officials suddenly awoke to some uncomfortable facts: buried under the picnic tables lay carcinogenic benzene and phenols, mercury and cyanide, coal tar distillates, and the lethal pesticide parathion. The opening of the park has been postponed indefinitely.

NIAGARA FALLS DISASTER

The time bomb effect of buried toxic substances was first perceived in the notorious case of the Love Canal. This gradual and cumulative disaster blighted a housing development, cost many families their homes, and, worst of all, destroyed the health and even the lives of many adults and children.

In 1894, William Love, a land developer with grandiose plans for a model city near Niagara Falls, began excavating a canal to connect the upper and lower levels of the Niagara River. By the time workers had dug a mile-long trench, 20 yards (18 m) wide and 11–40 feet (3–12 m) deep, Love ran out of interest and money. He abandoned the project. For some years, children used the half-dug canal as a swimming hole. Then the city, as well as several chemical companies, began using the trench as a burial place for waste products. From 1930 on, the final owners, Hooker Chemical Company, pitched in hundreds of fifty-five-gallon (209-l) drums filled with approximately eighty-two different toxic chemicals. Burying waste as "landfill" was considered acceptable practice at the time, and the chemical industry had little experience with the kinds of new compounds and the enormous quantities they were beginning to process.

In 1953, Hooker closed the trench with a clay cap, spread a thin layer of earth over it, and sold the land to the city of Niagara Falls for a token dollar. The city built a school and the beginnings of a playground on the flat field with its sparse, yellowish grass. A settlement of modest one-family homes grew up around it.

Now and then there were signs of trouble. Children and dogs who had rolled on the field developed skin rashes. In one back yard the ground gave way under a swimming pool and a blackish liquid with gleams of yellow and purple oozed to the surface. Slowly, as the underground drums rotted through, the earth began to collapse. Fence posts disintegrated, trees and bushes died.

At last, heavy rains penetrated the clay cap. It had been

damaged, in parts, by bulldozers digging building foundations and by the spreading roots of trees. Mixed with water, the chemicals leaked from the rotting drums and overflowed the canal trench at various points. In 1978, homes surrounding the site showed visible damage. Back yards and basements were filling with ill-smelling sludge. Worst of all, health problems now multiplied. Health Department investigators found some of the young married women suffering from miscarriages and birth abnormalities in their offspring. Residents were afflicted with liver abnormalities, rectal bleeding, skin rashes, and headaches. Children had severe throat and sinus ailments and were troubled with deafness. Air samples taken in basements of homes near the canal showed high concentrations of toxic compounds, including cancer causing benzene and chloroform.

One family whose members ate home-grown vegetables during their thirteen years of living near the canal experienced two miscarriages, birth defects in one child, one case of cancer, and a case of heart disease. Another family, whose basement had become inundated with toxic sludge, had a thirteen-year-old son who was born with an eye defect and later developed hearing trouble, an eleven-year-old daughter whose hair was falling out in clumps, and a nine-year-old daughter born with a defective heart, cleft palate, deformed nasal passages and ears, an enlarged liver, and a double row of teeth. The mother, too, suffered from a liver ailment.

In August 1978, President Carter conferred emergency status on the Love Canal area. The state of New York began evacuating residents whose houses were nearest the dump

**A young boy protests
the unhealthy conditions
caused by the chemicals in
Love Canal, located near
Niagara Falls, New York.**

site. Eventually, hundreds of families were forced to move away, and New York State paid more than $22 million to buy 237 of the affected homes and to begin cleaning up the former canal site.

Niagara Falls has been the home of a large number of chemical companies. All over town, investigations have turned up further dump sites, besides the one on the Love Canal. One of these is under the ball field of a school; a second one is only a few hundred feet from the city's water treatment plant. Near the campus of Niagara University, a 16-acre (6.5-hectare) former landfill containing the pesticides Mirex and lindane, has contaminated a small stream, Bloody Run Creek. Cats venturing near the creek are said to have lost teeth and patches of fur. In the water, no signs of life remain.

Probably the most lethal compounds lurking under the ground in Niagara County are trichlorophenol wastes, 37,000 tons in all, buried there between 1947 and 1972. The deadly dioxins contained in these wastes by far exceed those that exploded over the town of Seveso. Some 141 pounds (63.95 kg) of dioxin are said to be buried in the canal site and some 2,000 pounds (900 kg) elsewhere in the county. If this amount seems undramatic, one must bear in mind that according to scientific calculation three ounces (84 g) of dioxin are sufficient to kill one million people.

Recently, trace amounts of dioxin have been found in the leachate, or run-off water, that slowly drains from the old Love Canal landfill area. The presence of dioxin endangers the city's water supply. Worse than that, the Niagara River continues on into Lake Ontario which supplies water to the cities of Rochester, Syracuse, and Toronto.

SLOW SEEPAGE

Guarding against the poisoning of our drinking water has become a coast to coast struggle in recent years. Hazardous wastes buried in trenches or dumped into abandoned mines and quarries tend to leach out slowly. They join with rain water and drip into wells and streams. Communities situated miles downriver drink these invisible wastes in their coffee and tea or eat them in their fish and oysters. Farm animals who drink contaminated water give contaminated milk, and the milk, in turn, is made into contaminated cheese and butter. Meat, poultry, and eggs can also be affected.

In an Alabama village, for example, people who had nourished themselves for years on the local river fish turned out to have forty times the amount of the pesticide DDT in their body tissues than federal regulations permit for interstate shipment of meats. In the pine barrens of New Jersey, residents of a country town began suffering from rashes and kidney disease. One baby was born with kidney cancer. Investigators found benzene, chloroform, and other cancer causing substances in the water supply. Apparently, liquid wastes from a local landfill site had soaked through the sandy soil into the aquifer or water source. Although the landfill was officially closed to hazardous materials, so-called gypsy dumpers had managed to smuggle deadly chemical wastes past guards and inspectors.

Near Pittston, Pennsylvania, caustic and toxic chemicals secretly stashed in a maze of abandoned coal mines were discovered to be draining into the Susquehanna River. Sixty miles downstream, traces of dichlorobenzene, a suspected carcinogen, appeared in the drinking water.

MIDNIGHT DUMPING

In July 1978, a young Louisiana truck driver was told to pick up a truckload of alkaline-spent caustic (sodium hydroxide no longer useful to industry) and empty it quickly and secretly at an illegal dump site. As he began pouring out the caustic chemical, it combined with acids already present in the waste pond and caught him in a cloud of hydrogen sulfide gas. He was found dead at the site.

Gypsy or midnight dumping costs lives and causes severe environmental damage. What often happens is that small trucking firms, paid to get rid of hazardous wastes, simply do not know what to do with them or do not wish to pay for expensive disposal methods. That is why abandoned barrels full of unknown substances frequently turn up in the empty lots of cities or along the edges of country meadows. At night, trucks sometimes allow liquid wastes to dribble out along unlighted roads. Illegal dumpers pour chemicals into old quarries, unused wells, rented farm acreage, and city sewers. Even so-called legal dumping areas are often helter-skelter wastelands. Thousands of rotten and leaking containers spread across blighted acres have earned one dump site in Tennessee the name "Valley of the Drums." Such dumps are often called orphan sites, because no one feels responsible for them. No records exist of who dumped there and no one wants to clean them up. Altogether, government experts believe that only 10 percent of hazardous wastes are deposited in keeping with suggested federal regulations. Besides, the EPA has acknowledged that at present there simply are not enough legally adequate sites for dumping the rest.

TWO MILLION GALLONS OF TROUBLE

In 1970, American military forces stopped using the herbicide 2,4,5-T (Agent Orange) in spraying operations over Vietnam. Laboratory tests had shown that 2,4,5-T, always strongly contaminated with dioxin, is deadly to laboratory animals. This left the Air Force with a problem: how to cope with over 2 million gallons (7.6 million l) of surplus "Orange" without damaging human, animal, or plant life.

While 1.5 million steel drums full of the herbicide were slowly corroding on a Pacific island, some fifteen thousand were left to rust and leak at a naval installation in Mississippi. In a grim comedy that lasted seven years, officials debated where and how the leftover defoliant could safely be burned or buried. One state after another refused to admit the barrels. Cannisters of partially reprocessed dioxin were flown to several burial sites all over America, only to be turned back again. No one wanted the stuff around. At last, an international disposal company, owners of the incinerator ship Vulcanus, was given the job of ferrying the dreaded cargo to the central Pacific. There, in midocean, it was to be burned at ultra-high temperatures—around 1,645 degrees Centigrade (almost three thousand degrees Fahrenheit).

THE LIFE SPAN
OF HAZARDOUS WASTES

Toxic substances, such as PCBs and their chemical relatives, can be degraded by intense sunlight or high heat. But if they are left to lie quietly underground or underwater, they will remain unchanged, toxic to living organisms for decades, possibly even for centuries. A few substances—beryllium and cadmium, for example—remain highly toxic forever. They are stable metals which simply do not decay.

The heavy metal cadmium is used in plating steel, iron, and copper, in manufacturing glass, paints, storage batteries, insecticides, and a range of other products, and is present in motor vehicle exhaust. In 1971, milk from sixty-one American cities was found to contain seventeen to thirty parts per billion (ppb) of cadmium. This is a higher level than is considered acceptable in drinking water.

Newborn babies have almost no cadmium in their systems. Over the years, however, Americans are exposed to contaminated water supplies either from industrial wastes or from leaching of cadmium in galvanized copper pipes. Cigarettes, too, contain cadmium, which is inhaled with the smoke and retained by the body. By the age of fifty, the average American carries a burden of some thirty milligrams of cadmium. The metal tends to build up mainly in the kidneys and liver but also in the pancreas and blood vessels. Laboratory rats and mice who receive cadmium in their drinking water soon develop tumors and diseases of the kidneys, liver, and heart. Their life span is shortened. In humans, cadmium has been linked to high blood pressure, kidney damage, and prostate cancer.

A dramatic and terrible disease due to cadmium concentration in the body recently occurred in Japan. A cadmium mine released its wastes near a river also used to irrigate rice fields. After a few years of eating this rice, the local population, particularly the older women, began to feel dreadful pains in their backs and legs. Their bones became so distorted that the victims actually shrank in size and finally could no longer walk. The disease also made bones extremely brittle, so that fractures occurred at the slightest movement, even as a result of a cough or sneeze.

THE HILLS AT
MOUNTAIN VIEW

The white mineral, asbestos, is another substance that remains chemically unchanged. Its fibers enter the lungs and stay there, engendering cancer or other lung diseases, slowly, over a span of twenty or thirty years. Until recently, little was known about the effects of asbestos dust.

A few years ago, forty families settled at Mountain View Estates, an Arizona colony of mobile homes. When they first bought their property, they paid little attention to two huge, white, manmade hills that were part of the scenery.

"When the wind blows, you can see the stuff in the air," a home owner said angrily in an interview later on. She had learned that by constantly breathing the white dust from the hills she and other residents greatly increased the risk of developing cancer of the lungs, kidneys, or gastrointestinal system.

Next to the white hills stand the sheds of an abandoned asbestos mine. The mine wastes, piled up over the years, had created the hills. When the mine shut down in the 1970s, the owner used asbestos waste for landfill and sold off the entire area as housing lots. About 60 percent of the ground on which the new homes were placed consists of asbestos dust.

RADON DAUGHTERS

Back in 1921, Marie Curie, discoverer of radium, paid a visit to the United States. To honor the famous scientist, a group of American women raised $120,000 to purchase one gram

**Workers with special protective clothing and respirators
move asbestos dust dumped illegally at a site in Maryland.**

of radium as a gift to help her continue her research. Without realizing the cause, Madame Curie was already ill with the effects of radiation which would soon end her life. All the same, she traveled to Washington to receive her gift. In the East Room of the White House, President Harding handed her the gram of radium in a simple, unprotected vial.

Nowadays, a gram of radium would come packed in a metal containment vessel with 5 inch (12.70 cm) thick walls. The destructive effects of radium were not understood until forty years after radioactivity was discovered. The danger became clear only very slowly, with the growing number of deaths from cancer among radiation researchers, X-ray technicians, factory workers handling radium, and uranium miners.

As recently as 1950, radium was still used in cosmetics such as hair removers and gleaming eye shadow. Most commonly, it was applied to the numbers on watch dials to make them glow in the dark. The factories where these products were made were later sold to other businesses without regard for their continued high levels of radioactivity. Residues of radium enter the lungs in the form of radon gas. This odorless substance quickly decays into what are called radon daughters, radioactive particles which stay in the body, emitting further radiation that damages body tissues.

Recently, an entire industrial park in Pennsylvania was surveyed for radioactivity. The development was built on the site of a former center for extracting radium from Colorado uranium ore. Since it takes five tons of ore to make one precious gram of radium, mountains of radioactive wastes had been piling up all around the plant for decades.

The new owners of the factory site, along with some of their workers, received an unpleasant surprise when they heard from the U.S. Department of Energy that they were being bombarded by radiation from radon daughters, both from outside and from inside their bodies. The survey of buildings showed that workers were receiving radiation exposures up to fourteen times higher than the safety level set by the government.

POWER PLANT WASTES

The wastes from nuclear power plants are actually complex mixtures in which some particles last only a moment and others last thousands of years. At present, though, these high-level wastes, as they are called, have not yet made as destructive an impact on our environment as toxic wastes. That is because the volume of nuclear wastes is comparatively small. Since the beginning of the nuclear power era, only about five thousand metric tons of nuclear wastes have accumulated. On the other hand, all other industries combined now generate 100,000 times this tonnage of toxic wastes in just one year.

CHAPTER VII
MURKY WATERS

There was a time when rivers, lakes, and oceans seemed infinitely renewable. They served as bottomless sinks into which one could pour almost anything to make it disappear. Factories that needed plenty of water for washing and cooling during production were usually situated on the banks of lakes or rivers. This gave them the added convenience of being able to flush wastes straight into the water. It was hoped that the wastes would disintegrate on their way downstream, disperse, or come to rest on the bottom forever.

Some of the dirtiest industrial wash water comes from steel mills. Tons of metallic particles, acids, oils, and poisons, such as phenol, ammonia, and cyanide, are emitted in steel making. Though steel plants make an effort to clean and reuse the vast quantities of water they need, an estimated 50 percent of the harmful waste substances end up getting flushed downriver.

Textile finishing is another industry that pours out far dirtier water than it takes in. Cancer causing dyes, salt, and organic particles drain into the nation's streams by the millions of pounds each year.

Paper manufacturing, too, soaks up water in trillions of gallons, then spews it back brown and foaming and full of sludge, bleaching chemicals, wood sugars, and mercury used as a fungus preventive. One venerable old paper mill has built up a 300 acre (120 hectare) sludge mat, 12 feet (3.6 m) thick, on the bottom of Lake Champlain.

Dozens of other industries pour wastes into the water virtually untreated. Among the smallest, but by far not the cleanest, are poultry butchering concerns that dump chicken heads, feathers, blood, and intestines into local streams to decompose, spreading festering odors for miles around.

PCBs IN THE HUDSON

In contrast to such obvious pollutants as rotting chicken heads, other harmful substances are odorless and leave no unsightly traces in the water. This is true of the polychlorinated biphenyls (PCBs), a group of chemicals which seemed, for years, to disappear harmlessly.

PCB, developed in the 1930s, was welcomed by manufacturers of electrical equipment as a new miracle substance. It is used to raise the efficiency of electrical conductors in everything from toasters to mammoth generators—wall coverings and fabrics, insulating tapes, lacquers, envelope adhesives, hydraulic fluids, fireproofing compounds, and scores of other familiar products. The great advantage of PCBs is that they are almost totally resistant to fire or explosion.

In appearance, PCB is a heavy, brown liquid without much odor. Discharged into water it sinks straight to the bottom. It does not cause sudden death to swarms of fish. The chemical seems so harmless that for nearly fifty years it was worldwide industrial practice to discharge it into waterways or to dump it in landfill.

Still, there were a few warning signs. As early as 1943, the New York State Department of Labor investigated two cable manufacturing plants using chlorinated biphenyls.

Several deaths due to liver damage and severe cases of the skin disease, chloracne, had been reported among workers.

In two General Electric Company plants on the Hudson River, sixty-five employees working with PCBs had become ill over a fifteen-year period. They suffered from skin rashes, nausea, asthmatic bronchitis, and eye irritations. In spite of this, General Electric's two plants continued to discharge 25 to 30 pounds (about 11 to 14 kg) of PCBs into the Hudson River every day.

PCBs were in use for about thirty years before anyone realized that they were polluting the surroundings. A Swedish scientist made this discovery while searching for residues of the pesticide DDT in wildlife and human fat. He was working on the theory that pesticides might be causing the decline of the seal population in the Baltic Sea. What he found instead, though, were traces of an unknown substance. He began to track it down and eventually discovered it to be PCB.

Soon, analyses by American scientists followed. In 1968, an accident was publicized, in which a machine part broke in a Japanese food processing plant, spilling PCB into a batch of rice oil. About one thousand persons were severely poisoned. Eight years after the accident, numerous deaths from liver cancer occurred among the victims.

For some years, also, American mink ranchers had been reporting that their female minks were not reproducing properly. Mink, of course, live on a steady diet of fish. By 1972, it had been shown that salmon from Lake Ontario were heavily contaminated by PCBs. As for fish from the Hudson River, they contained PCBs in their flesh and in their eggs —an average of 11.4 parts per billion (ppb) in the eggs and 4.01 parts per million (ppm) in their flesh. A few years later, several Hudson River fish were found to have 100 ppm of PCBs in their edible flesh, and two Environmental Protection officers came upon a rock bass measuring in at 355 ppm. Concentrations of PCB, like those of the pesticide DDT, increase (bioaccumulate) in the food chain.

The Food and Drug Administration (FDA), new to the problem of PCBs, established a temporary tolerance limit of five ppm for fish. In August of 1975, newspapers issued public warnings against eating salmon from Lake Ontario and striped bass from the Hudson. Since fish in the Hudson exceeded the human tolerance level set by the FDA it was necessary to close the river to commercial and sport fishing.

In 1976, New York State's Department of Environmental Conservation found the General Electric Company (GE) guilty of violating state water quality standards. The decision read in part: "PCBs are toxic substances capable in sufficient quantities of causing skin lesions, destroying cells in vital body organs, adversely affecting reproduction, and inducing cancer and death."

General Electric has stopped discharging PCBs and has, in fact, substituted another material considered safer in its products. Unfortunately, 440,000 pounds (200,000 kg) of lethal PCBs still lie at the bottom of the Hudson River. GE agreed in 1976 to pay a bill of $7 million to New York State for cleaning up the river and to set aside one million more for research on pollution and waste disposal. Large as it seems, this sum of money is not enough for the task.

Not one of the clean-up methods experts have suggested seems entirely satisfactory. Harvesting the saturated fish and incinerating them at high temperatures would take care of only a fraction of the problem. Since they lie under water, PCBs can neither be soaked up with mats nor neutralized with ultraviolet rays. Decay bacteria will not touch them. The only possible clean-up method would be to dredge the toxic muck to the surface with expensive special equipment. And even dredging presents problems. It would certainly stir up PCBs lying dormant below and set them afloat in the currents to be ingested by fish and shellfish and thus to enter the food chain. Finally, dredging means that a place would have to be found for depositing hundreds of thousands of tons of PCB-contaminated mud, without bringing pollution into clean territory.

While the debate goes on, swarms of herring, bass, and shad will come in from the sea each spring to head up the Hudson for their spawning grounds. They will pick up PCB on their way, and it will accumulate in their bodies. They will lay their millions of eggs and, later, their offspring will pick up PCB on their way downriver and will spread the contamination far beyond their place of birth.

PCB pollution has become a worldwide problem. In the Baltic Sea where there were known to be some twenty thousand seals in 1940, only a few thousand remain. Sea birds on the coast of England were discovered carrying PCB residues in the liver ranging up to 9,590 ppm. In 1970, 146,000 chickens had to be destroyed in New York State when a prominent soup manufacturing company found high levels of PCBs in the meat. In 1971, fifty thousand turkeys were taken off the market by the Food and Drug Administration for the same reason.

Among humans, the highest concentrations of PCBs in the fatty tissues are found in residents of industrial areas. The EPA estimates that half the people living in the United States carry from one to three parts per million PCBs, and that we keep accumulating more. A 1975 nationwide study conducted by EPA found that nearly one third of all nursing mothers' milk contained PCB.

Under the Toxic Substances Control Act the manufacture, processing, and sale of PCBs was prohibited in the United States after 1979. Much damage has already been done, though. Millions of PCB-containing electrical parts are still in use all over the world. Eventually, as they begin to malfunction, they will end up on the nearest waste disposal dump. Eventually, too, they will crack and spill their toxic contents to be washed into the soil by rain or to mingle with dust and be carried away by the wind.

Help may be on the way, however. Recently, the Goodyear Company applied for patents on a process designed to convert PCBs into non-toxic substances. The company claims the technique will reduce the risk, time, and cost of PCB disposal.

KEPONE IN THE JAMES

River dumping of toxic materials can cost the manufacturer millions of dollars. Beginning in the 1950s, Allied Chemical Company produced Kepone, a deadly pesticide used mainly against the European potato beetle. Allied farmed out the job of producing Kepone to a subcontractor, a smaller company in Pennsylvania. This company was careless in its housekeeping. Workers were often seen on the job without gloves or masks and even took their lunch boxes into the workroom which was laden with Kepone dust. Within a few years, a group of workers became ill. Their hands trembled and their eyes rolled involuntarily. They suffered from violent headaches and several of the men were found to be sterile. Even some of their wives and children at home had Kepone in their blood. The factory building was too full of Kepone dust to be detoxified. Clean-up crews had to take the machinery apart and place the pieces in a sealed pit.

During the investigation of this case, EPA officials discovered that Allied Chemical had also been secretly discharging Kepone wastes into the James River which runs into Chesapeake Bay. The James had to be closed to fishing and oystering. It was later reopened, then closed once again.

Altogether, the company received a multi-million-dollar bill in lawsuits from workers, fishermen, stockholders, and the state of Virginia. It turned out that company managers had kept their river dumping a secret because they were afraid the EPA would force them to install water treatment equipment costing about $700,000.

Kepone production has now been banned in the United States, and no other countries produce the substance either. Like PCBs, though, Kepone has settled to the bottom of the river, and no decision has been reached as to the best method for removing it.

THE GREAT LAKES

It took less than a hundred years of human interference to destroy the ecological balance of the world's largest group of fresh-water lakes. Overfishing and the opening of shipping canals between the lakes hastened the extinction of the native fish population. Then mining companies and other industries settled on the banks. They used the lakes as both their water source and their sewer.

On Lake Superior, for example, the Reserve Mining Company daily discharged thousands of tons of ore wastes, or tailings, into the water. It was discovered that the tailings, damaging enough in themselves, also contained a high percentage of asbestos fibers. In 1980, a successful legal fight finally halted this dumping which had been going on for twenty-five years. By now, though, asbestos fibers are suspended throughout the lake. The city of Duluth and other Minnesota communities were forced to install special filtering equipment to remove the fibers from their drinking water. No one knows how many people ingested asbestos before its presence was detected.

There is some cause for rejoicing, however. Since the ban on spraying the pesticide DDT, residues in Great Lakes fish are disappearing faster than experts had predicted. Observers now estimate that within twenty-five years all fish in the lakes will be completely free of this dangerous chemical.

MINAMATA DISEASE

Heavy metals in water are just as dangerous as in air, and even more common. An infamous case of public mercury poisoning was discovered in Japan in the 1960s. In the island town of Minamata, a chemical factory produced mercury among other substances. In 1953, townspeople noticed cats and dogs dying of convulsions. Many local fishermen, too, suffered from convulsions, numbness, trembling, and other disturbances of the nervous system.

Investigators found that mercury wastes discharged into Minamata Bay by the chemical plant had become more and more concentrated in the local shellfish, which were a popular and inexpensive food. Since then, over seven hundred citizens have developed symptoms of brain damage such as blindness, palsy, and mental disorders. An unusual number of malformed children have been born, and more than a hundred victims have died.

Closer to home, Minamata disease has recently been diagnosed in several Indian settlements in Canada. The streams which run through the territory have been contaminated by mercury from mining companies and wood pulp bleaching plants. Since 1970, high levels of mercury have been found in the local fish. For the Indians, this is disastrous. Fishing is a vital part of their lives, and fish is their main source of protein. The announcement that the fish are poisoned has confused and angered the Indians. They have found it hard to believe that this is really true, because the first signs of Minamata disease—trembling hands, numb extremities, headache, and constricted vision—have shown up in only a few cases. These symptoms can take as long as ten years to appear.

OIL IN THE OCEANS

A tanker is burning at sea. It has been aflame for a week, and each hour some 10,000 gallons (38,000 l) of petroleum pour from its side into the ocean. Even so, the ship, which holds 70 million gallons (266 million l), is still three-quarters full. Firefighters have stopped trying to extinguish the blaze until they can bring more chemicals and equipment to the scene. When the fire is finally put out, it may take as long as six more weeks to transfer the remaining oil to other tankers. The death toll, incidentally, from this particular two-ship collision which occurred in 1979, was twenty-seven crewmen.

Such accidents are common. As many as 240 million gallons (912 million l) of petroleum are imported into the United States each day. Even though modern tankers are gigantic, only an inch (25 mm) thick skin of steel separates the precious black mud in the hold from the saltwater outside. Every year, U.S. waters are polluted by more than 10 million gallons (38 million l) of oil, lost in more than ten thousand spills. These accidents leave behind hundreds of dead birds, grease-smeared harbors, blackened beaches, and fish that taste of petroleum. Oil spills harm plant and animal life of the underwater shoreline and cause considerable economic hardship to people in coastal towns. Cleaning up after the spill is cumbersome and expensive. It is especially difficult in cold climates, such as that of Alaska, where the oil may congeal and even solidify.

SPILLS AND BLOWOUTS

The first of the mammoth oil spills occurred in the wreck of the Torrey Canyon. She was an early supertanker, built in 1959 to hold 66,000 tons. A few years later, she was "jumboized" in Japan to hold twice that amount. In 1967, coming from the Persian Gulf and heading for port in England, she became stuck on a reef in the English Channel. She clung there immovable for six weeks, despite efforts to set her afire by bombing her from the air. Thirty-six million gallons (136 million l) of Kuwaiti crude oil poured from her hulk, billowed in the water, and laid its black grease across the beaches of Cornwall.

Eleven years later, an even larger tanker, the Amoco Cadiz, foundered near the coast of France and spread a monstrous, 60 million gallon (228 million l) oil blob over French fishing villages, harbors, and beaches.

Ships alone are not responsible for oil spilled at sea. In 1969, a high-pressure offshore well blew out near Santa Barbara, California. Oil continued to leak for almost a year and caused several million dollars' damage. Then, in the summer of 1979, Ixtoc I, an offshore well in the Gulf of Mexico blew out, creating the largest oil spill of all times. It vented at a

An offshore oil rig spews oil into the air causing a trail of pollution to wind into the Gulf of Mexico in March, 1970.

rate of some thirty thousand barrels a day. In spite of desperate efforts to cap the well, crude oil flowed unchecked for nine months before experts could even slow it down. A hundred miles of Texas coastline were fouled, but much of the oil washed out to sea or came to rest in fudgy globules on the offshore Texas barrier islands. Planes flew out to spray the larger floating oil patches with detergent chemicals to dissolve them. The largest slick was 12 miles (19.2 km) long and half a mile (.80 km) across.

Unfortunately, some of the measures taken to clean up spilled oil are in themselves harmful to marine life. Burning oil at sea, of course, raises acrid clouds of smoke. Sinking the floating oil with sand and chalk is a method often used in Europe. This deposits oil on the sea bottom where it settles permanently into the sediment. In coastal waters this can damage shellfish and the kind of sea life that supports commercial fisheries. Mopping up shores with straw or peat moss is not especially damaging, but it is a messy job. Cleaning the shoreline with hot steam, or with detergents, causes definite biological damage. Mixtures of solvents and petroleum, too, tend to be quite toxic and dangerous to sea birds and mammals.

Some oiled shorelines recover within weeks, while others may take ten years to return to normal. On the whole, little is known about the long-range effects of petroleum on life near the shore. Even less is known about the impact of acres of floating oil globs on the high seas. It is probable that they affect young fish as well as the tiny organisms that larger fish require for their nourishment.

Scientists do know that oil can kill marine birds, fish, and shellfish through coating and asphyxiation, poisoning by contact, or ingestion, destruction of food sources, and by chemically disrupting the clues these creatures follow in feeding and reproduction.

RADIOACTIVE OCEAN DUMPING

In 1970, the United States ended its practice of dumping low-level nuclear wastes into the ocean. By that time, thou-

Young people help spread hay to soak up the oil after an offshore oil rig burned near Galveston, Texas.

sands of 55 gallon (209 l) drums were scattered across four sea bed disposal areas—two in the Atlantic, two in the Pacific.

During the early decades of nuclear development, specialized disposal companies embedded these wastes in concrete, encased them in steel containers, ferried them out to sea, and dropped them overboard in designated areas. More recently, experts have agreed that it is better to contain such wastes in the smallest possible space than to disperse them widely. Burial on land rather than at sea is now preferred.

Several European countries, though, are still burying radioactive wastes in the ocean. They are supervised by the International Atomic Energy Agency which grants permits for dumping properly packaged low level wastes. Sea disposal of high-level wastes is altogether prohibited. Because of the possible harm that may come from radioactive leakage, and because ocean dumping is very expensive, most European countries are now looking for new disposal sites on land.

Too little is known about the impact of nuclear wastes on ocean life. In 1974, the American Office of Radiation Programs of the EPA set out to inspect some of the radioactive waste packages dropped into the sea some fifteen years before. Using submersibles, some unmanned and some occupied by observers, scientists scanned the ocean floor, took photographs, and collected sediment from around the drums for laboratory analysis. They found elevated plutonium levels in the immediate vicinity of the drums. When it came to pinpointing a particular effect on sea life, though, they found that the presence of many other pollutants confused the issue. Wastes such as explosives, toxics, and heavy metals, all harmful in various ways, are also present in ocean waters.

If future generations of Americans return to depositing nuclear wastes in the ocean, they will probably work at deeper levels than before, 4,000 feet (1,220 m) and more below the surface, where food fish do not circulate.

On the whole, sea bed disposal for nuclear wastes has many advantages. Changes are very slow on the ocean floor. Deposits accumulate gradually, sifting down to cover objects below, and there is little turbulence or erosion. Indeed, there are large parts of the ocean bottom in which nothing seems to have changed for fifty million years.

CHAPTER VIII
NUCLEAR ENERGY

Nuclear power plants have become an important source of energy both in America and abroad. More than sixty operating plants supply some fifty thousand megawatts of electricity in the United States alone. There is little doubt that there are tremendous benefits to be derived from nuclear power. It is also quite clear that accidents at nuclear plants are possible. There may be hazards to the general population and to the biosphere. This has led to controversy over the measures taken by electric power companies to insure proper safety.

Although a reactor cannot explode like an atom bomb, there nevertheless are hazards associated with both the intense radiation within the reactor itself and the possible release to the community of the radioactive material it contains.

CHAIN REACTION
In a nuclear fission power reactor, the source of energy is the conversion of mass into energy during the splitting or "fissioning" of uranium-235 into two lighter elements. The fission is triggered by the absorption of a neutron, one of the fundamental particles that make up the nucleus of atoms.

On the average, the fissioning of 2.2 lbs (1 kg) of uranium will produce about the same amount of energy as the burning of thirteen thousand barrels of oil or twenty-five hundred tons of coal.

The threat posed by the tremendous amount of radioactivity in a nuclear power plant is ever present. A typical operating power plant will contain fifteen billion Curies of activity produced by its fission products. A Curie (named after Madame Curie who discovered radium) is a basic unit of radioactivity equivalent to 37 billion atoms disintegrating per second. The activity represented by the fission products of an operating reactor is equivalent to that of 33 million pounds (roughly 15 million kg) of radium.

In the 1960s, the Atomic Energy Commission estimated that the release of half of the fission products of a working reactor would result in the death of several thousand people from acute radiation exposure. The commission also pointed out, though, that the chances of this happening were only one in one billion years of operating life for a reactor.

The tremendous number of neutrons present in a reactor are an additional hazard, since neutrons are extremely damaging to biological systems. To aggravate matters, neutrons absorbed by most other materials render these radioactive also. This is called neutron activation. Many of the structural materials of the reactor thus become radioactive during the course of its operation. Even the uranium-238 becomes activated and forms a whole series of exotic elements known as transuranium elements or "actinides." One of these actinides is plutonium-239, an extremely toxic substance that is also used in the production of nuclear weapons.

NUCLEAR ACCIDENTS

The safety record of the nuclear power industry is, on the whole, impressive. There have been no identifiable deaths associated with accidents in American commercial reactors. There have been accidents, however, and one, on Three Mile Island, Pennsylvania, was serious enough to endanger the future of nuclear energy in this country.

Earlier, in 1952, an accident occurred at Chalk River, Ontario. Due to human error, the opening of improper valves led to a small gas explosion that destroyed the core of the reactor. The safety system functioned properly and no radioactivity escaped.

A fire at the Windscale Reactor on the coast of northern England, in 1957, caused the release of some radioactivity to the environment. Large areas of the North Sea became contaminated, and milk supplies from miles of grazing land surrounding the reactor site had to be dumped.

In yet another accident, a break in a metal plate at the Fermi breeder reactor near Detroit nearly caused a major disaster. Officials later stated that some "hair-raising decisions had to be made." Some melting of fuel elements did occur, but fortunately there was no release of radioactivity.

A fire at the Brown's Ferry nuclear power plant in Alabama stimulated a flurry of public attention to the question of nuclear safety. The fire was caused by poor design and almost resulted in the meltdown of a large part of the fuel. Again, safety systems, operating properly, prevented a major accident.

THREE MILE ISLAND
On March 28, 1979, several water pumps stopped working in the nuclear power plant called TMI-2 at Three Mile Island, Pennsylvania. So began an accident that was to be unique in the history of the United States. Millions of people were threatened by what had happened and thousands were confronted with the possibility of evacuation. Newspapers ran headlines about dangerous releases of radiation that would make the area unfit for habitation for thousands of years. To understand how so much fear and uncertainty could be generated, we need to take a closer look at the operation of a reactor.

FISSION PRODUCT HEAT
An unavoidable byproduct of the fissioning of uranium are the highly radioactive and long-lived fission products. They are the cause of a number of the problems associated with

the use of nuclear energy. These products accumulate in the reactor and great care has to be taken to prevent their escape to the surrounding environment. To make matters worse, they themselves give off so much energy in the form of heat that the reactor must be cooled even after shutdown to prevent damage to the fuel. The intense radiation is so great from these fission residues that certain parts of the reactor are inaccessible even when the reactor is not functioning.

MODERATOR

In order to sustain a chain reaction, one of the neutrons emitted by a fissioning uranium nucleus must be absorbed by another uranium nucleus. The efficiency of this process is greatly increased by first slowing the neutron down. It is similar, in a way, to the greater ease of catching a slow moving ball rather than a fast one. Present-day commercial reactors take advantage of this by containing a moderator, usually water, to slow or moderate the neutrons through the many collisions with water molecules. There is the added advantage that water can be used as a coolant as well.

REACTOR CORE

The heart of the power plant is the reactor core. The core at Three Mile Island (TMI-2) contained about 100 tons of uranium dioxide (UO_2) in the form of small cylindrical pellets, about one-half inch (12.5 mm) in diameter and one inch (25 mm) long. The pellets were loaded inside fuel rods, each about 12 feet (3.60 m) long. The rods were then spaced in the form of a cylindrical lattice. The spacing is important since it must allow the moderator and coolant water to flow between the rods and also permit access to various testing instruments that measure temperature and radiation levels.

Control rods also enter the core through these spaces. The rods are made of materials such as silver and cadmium, which strongly absorb neutrons. When they are lowered into the fuel assembly they effectively stop or slow the chain reaction. In an emergency, the rods are designed to "scram," that is automatically to drop into the core.

CONTAINMENT

For added safety the reactor core is contained within a 40-foot (12-m) high steel tank called the reactor vessel. The walls of this vessel are 8 feet (2.40 meters) thick. Water enters the reactor vessel at a temperature of 288 degrees C (550 degrees F) and, after being heated, leaves at about 318 degrees C (600 degrees F). The water in the type of reactor found at TMI enters at a very high pressure, about 2,100 pounds (954 kg) per square inch (psi) to prevent boiling and forming of bubbles. (Normal atmospheric pressure is 14.7 pounds [6.62 kg] psi.)

As exotic as it may appear, a reactor is basically a way of heating water to make steam which will, eventually, drive a turbine to turn a generator to make electricity. As soon as the water leaves the reactor, the system becomes similar to that of any conventional power plant. The water flows through a steam generator and heats the "feed water" in a separate set of pipes to make steam. The water then continues through a pressurizer to maintain it at the required pressure. As in other power plants, the system ends in a tower to cool the spent steam after it leaves the turbine and send it back to the reactor.

As a final added safety measure the reactor vessel, steam generator, and pressurizer are confined within another containment building, a reinforced concrete structure 193 feet (about 58 m) high, with walls 4 feet (1.2 m) thick, to protect the public from the effects of an accident. Of course, the instrument panel through which workers control the reactor is in a separate building, a short distance away.

THE "TRIP"

At 4:00 A.M. on March 28, the pumps that supply feed water to the steam generator tripped. To an engineer, a "trip" means that a piece of machinery stops working. There was no water to be heated into steam. The automatic safety system immediately shut down the turbine and electric generator.

The temperature of the reactor coolant began rising, since it no longer was losing its heat in making steam. It expanded and the pressure began to build up. This caused a relief valve at the top of the pressurizer to open, permitting some steam and water from the coolant to drain through a pipe to a holding tank on the floor of the containment building. The pressure kept rising, however, and eight seconds after the trip, the control rods dropped and the reactor scrammed. So far, everything operated as planned.

The generation of heat did not stop, though. The fission products were still there and their energy release in the form of heat was unstoppable. Ordinarily, when the main feedwater system is blocked, there are emergency feedwater pumps that automatically start. Operators in the control room apparently did not notice two lights that should have warned them that closed valves blocked each of the emergency feedwater lines and that absolutely no water was reaching the steam generator. One light was covered with a yellow maintenance tag. Why the other light was not noticed is not known.

LOCA

A loss of coolant flow through the reactor can have very serious consequences for the entire plant. Engineers call this a LOCA or Loss of Cooling Accident. The absence of coolant would cause the fuel rods to melt because of fission products heating. The molten fuel coming into contact with any remaining water in the vessel would initiate chemical reactions that would produce, among other things, more heat and very explosive hydrogen gas. In time, the whole molten mass could melt through the vessel and even through the concrete beneath the containment building, and then sink into the earth. This phenomenon is often referred to as the China Syndrome, presumably because the molten mass would eventually burrow its way through the earth and reach China.

A breach of the containment vessel, even if it did not lead to anything quite so dramatic, would result in the release of radioactive fission products. To guard against such a core meltdown, the reactor is designed with an emergency core cooling system (ECCS). The ECCS functions to replace the lost primary coolant.

STUCK VALVE

Some thirteen seconds after the scram, the relief valve should have closed. But the valve stuck open, and it would remain open for some two-and-a-half hours. Essential coolant was being lost to the drain tank. A LOCA was in progress. Confusion over mixed signals at the control panel led the operators to shut off the ECCS prematurely.

Steam began forming in the reactor vessel itself, which increased the pressure so that more water was displaced through the relief valve. The drain tank filled and overflowed into the sump (that is, the pit where excess liquid collects) at the bottom of the building. From the sump it was pumped to a waste storage tank in an auxiliary building. Within one-half hour from the start of the accident, as much as 3,000 gallons (11,400 l) of slightly radioactive water had been drained.

RADIATION AREA

Radiation levels were increasing throughout the plant. Evidence began accumulating that some of the reactor's fuel rod cladding had burst, permitting radioactive gases to escape into the coolant water. With the top of the core uncovered, the temperature rose to the point, 1,200 degrees C (2,200 degrees F) at which the zirconium alloy used in the cladding was reacting with the steam to produce hydrogen.

When the radiation level within the containment building rose to 800 rems per hour (according to regulations, a worker is not permitted more than five rems per year) a general emergency was declared at Three Mile Island. The containment building was automatically isolated some four hours after the accident. Although designed to prevent radioactive material from leaking into the environment, some of the coolant water flowed to an auxiliary building. Some of the small amount of radioactivity ultimately released occurred here.

Off the island, air sample readings found no iodine-131. This gaseous radioactive isotope of iodine is of concern because it is the one fission product that is easily absorbed through breathing and that concentrates in the body. It accumulates in the thyroid gland, either through breathing or through drinking milk.

State officials only learned of the accident at Three Mile Island through the news media. Finally, at 9:15 A.M., still on Wednesday the twenty-eighth, the White House was notified. It was not until 2:00 P.M. Friday that senior officials of the Nuclear Regulatory Commission (NRC) arrived at TMI, bringing a dozen experts from NRC headquarters.

THE BIG BUBBLE

There was a release of some radiation the next morning, Thursday the twenty-ninth. A helicopter flying over the vent stack of TMI-2 observed a reading of 1,200 millirem per hour. It was a controlled release of gases that was building up pressure in the storage tank in the auxiliary building. Communication between the TMI staff and the NRC was so confused, by this time, that when word of the release reached NRC officials they were not informed of its source. The general concern and apprehension of the NRC officials prompted them to recommend evacuation of the area. After some discussion, Governor Richard Thornburgh of Pennsylvania recommended that pregnant women and preschool children leave the region within a five-mile radius of Three Mile Island and that all schools in the area be closed.

Many people quietly evacuated on their own. The three counties closest to TMI made plans to evacuate their residents living within a radius of five miles of the reactor, some twenty-five thousand people. Officials were asked to develop twenty-mile evacuation plans. Drug and bottle manufacturers went on a crash program to produce and supply some

237,000 bottles of potassium iodide. Taken in large doses, this drug saturates the thyroid gland so that if a person were to be exposed to radioactive iodine, the thyroid gland would not be able to absorb it. Emergency supplies of this drug were kept under armed guard in a Harrisburg warehouse but were never distributed.

A new problem presented itself. A large bubble of hydrogen gas was forming in the vessel. The source of the hydrogen was the reaction between steam at high temperature and the zirconium cladding of the fuel rods. There was now apparently the potential for a large explosion. The major question was whether there was enough oxygen present for combustion. The source of oxygen was thought to be radiolysis, a process whereby radiation breaks apart water molecules into its components, hydrogen and oxygen. The possibility of such an explosion rupturing the containment vessel and spewing forth deadly radioactivity captured news headlines for several days. It now appears, though, that the concern over such a catastrophic explosion was groundless.

COLD SHUTDOWN

Cold Shutdown, when the temperature of the reactor coolant water fell below the boiling point, marked the end of the crisis. A sense of normalcy finally returned to the area surrounding TMI-2. But the after effects of the accident are still with us. There are still a million gallons of radioactive water in the containment building. There is a badly damaged and highly radioactive reactor core. The clean-up process, decontamination, disposal of 1 million gallons (3.8 million l) of radioactive water and solid radioactive debris, as well as the reconstruction required to put TMI-2 back on line again, have been estimated to cost in the neighborhood of $2 billion and will present their own health hazards. Further releases of radioactive gases will probably be necessary. The total release of radioactivity to the environment from March 28 to April 7 has been estimated as 13 to 17 Curies of iodine and 2.4 million to 13 million Curies of radioactive noble gases, mainly Krypton.

The Report of the President's Commission on the Accident at TMI concluded that this released radiation would have a negligible effect on the health of the 2 million individuals living within fifty miles of the island.

NUCLEAR WASTES

One of the most difficult problems associated with nuclear power occurs at the end of the lifetime of the fuel. After a year or so in the reactor, the fuel elements have accumulated so many fission products that they effectively "poison" the chain reaction. This spent fuel, millions of times more radioactive than the original uranium it contained, must be removed. Usually it is removed and stored underwater near the plant itself. Storage space, however, is limited.

Ideally, the next step should be "fuel reprocessing." Here, the fuel rods would be shipped to a chemical plant, carefully dissolved, and the unused uranium-235 together with the valuable plutonium-239 removed from the other wastes. The unwanted waste would be packaged and disposed of at a carefully chosen site. Reprocessing could thus greatly increase the amount of available nuclear fuel.

A decision by the Carter administration has led to a moratorium on all reactor fuel reprocessing in the United States. This decision was prompted by fear of nuclear weapon proliferation using the recovered plutonium as well as based on the opinion that no safe nuclear repository was available for the waste.

HOLDING PATTERN

At present there are over a million gallons of "high level" radioactive wastes stored in about two hundred huge underground tanks at the Hanford Works on the Columbia River in the state of Washington, and at the Savannah River Plant in South Carolina. These wastes were generated by the nuclear weapons program. The fission product activity of these bomb-produced waste products is about 600 million Curies.

These tanks have a life of only about twenty years. Corrosion and radiation damage cause them to buckle and leak. There have been nine failures to date. One was not discovered until some 60,000 gallons (about 227,000 l) of highly radioactive liquid leaked into the soil and the river.

Failing a decision for national nuclear waste disposal and reprocessing, there is no solution to this problem. One plan was to build new tanks and transfer the waste every twenty years, generation after generation.

Spent fuel continues to accumulate in the United States. Eventually, the problem of what to do with it will have to be faced. Evidence is mounting that safe and reliable management of nuclear wastes can be accomplished. Engineers have made great progress in developing techniques for "calcining" liquid wastes into solid form for easier handling. Calcination is basically just the heating of liquid droplets in air to form a dry powder or granules. By chemical means, the calcine is then transformed into a material resembling glass or ceramic. This stable material, further encased in thick steel cans, would then be buried deep underground in some stable geological formation such as a salt bed or granitic rock.

One objection to this disposal method that has been raised, though, is that the heat generated by the wastes would alter these geological formations and affect their stability.

Other plans are also being considered for storing the spent fuel without processing. Since the fission products are actually immobilized in the fuel pellet cladding, the fuel could simply be stored for long periods at "retrievable surface storage" sites. An advantage to retrievability is that the fuel could later be reprocessed to recover valuable fuel.

The Energy Research and Development Administration (ERDA) is discussing waste-processing problems with several countries, including Germany, France, Sweden, and the United Kingdom. It is now planned to construct six terminal storage facilities in salt formations. The first two plants are scheduled to receive waste in the middle of 1985. The other plants will start operating at two-year intervals. Even though the NRC is still developing its regulations, standards, and guides in this field, there should be no scientific barrier to a safe repository for waste in the near future.

THE "FRONT" END
OF THE FUEL CYCLE

We have discussed the problem of dealing with spent fuel—at, what is called, the end of the fuel cycle. But there are also hazards associated with the beginning of the fuel cycle. The "front" end of the cycle is when the uranium ore is processed into useful fuel. Surprisingly, it accounts for the most significant releases of radioactivity, much more than an operating power plant itself. Miners and other workers are exposed to radiation at the mine site as well as at the milling operations where the crude ore is converted into high-purity uranium oxide for use in reactors.

The most important occupational hazard in uranium mining is due to radon-222 and its radioactive decay products, the radon daughters. Radon is a chemically inert gas, but one which can easily be inhaled and cause damage to the tissues and cells of the lungs and respiratory tract. Polonium-218, one of the radon daughters, is particularly troublesome since, unlike the radon, it is also chemically active and will attach itself to almost anything.

The very process of separating the uranium from its ore at the mills also produces wastes. These residues, or tailings, are dumped into huge piles near the mills. They also pose a threat to the environment since it is impossible to separate all the uranium and its daughters from the crude ore, so that the tailings themselves are radioactive.

The use of tailings as landfill under homes, stores, and schools increases their potential hazard. Houses built on such landfill in a development in Grand Junction, Colorado, were found to have radon concentrations that exceeded by a hundred times the allowable limits suggested by the Surgeon General of the United States.

Strong guidelines have recently been established to limit the use of tailings for construction purposes.

CHAPTER IX
CONSUMER PRODUCTS: SOME RUDE SURPRISES

Chemical pollution not only reaches us through the air we breathe and the water we drink, but at times, it also follows us all the way home from the grocery shelf. Between 1973 and 1975, for example, millions of unsuspecting consumers ate farm products contaminated with a fireproofing chemical. At about the same time, the familiar household material, asbestos, was found to be potently carcinogenic. Then, in yet another unpleasant surprise, scientists discovered that spray cans, used for everything from paint to cooking oil, contained a gas that could permanently destroy the earth's protective layer of ozone.

A FOOD CHAIN ACCIDENT: PBB

It was a grim year for cows in the state of Michigan. One farmer after another was forced to hire earth-moving machinery, dig a long, deep trench, lead his terrified dairy cattle to the burial place and shoot them one by one. The animals were sick and looked it. Their fur was in patches, their skin full of sores, their hooves large and misshapen, and their joints creaking. Most of them had long ago stopped giving milk. They had not been able to give birth, either, or had borne sick calves that quickly died.

The sickness had begun some time in 1973. It took farmers, veterinarians, and chemists many months before the cause was finally brought to light and officially recognized. By that time, hundreds of animals were dead and several families had lost their farms. Local people who had eaten their own dairy products were suffering from swollen limbs and joints, stomach and liver problems, headaches, and constant tiredness. Little children had painfully enlarged knees.

FIREMASTER
AND NUTRIMASTER

It was a case of carelessness and confusion, almost equally shared by the Michigan Chemical Company and the Michigan Farm Bureau's cooperative feed-mixing plant. In 1973, Michigan Chemical produced a new feed additive for dairy herds, a mixture called Nutrimaster. Nutrimaster consisted chiefly of magnesium oxide, recently in great demand by dairy farmers because it helps cows give more milk and makes the milk richer in butterfat. Nutrimaster came in 50-pound (22.68-kg) brown bags with the name clearly stenciled across the front.

At the same time, though, the factory also produced polybrominated biphenyl (PBB) a flame retardant of great efficiency but doubtful safety. Two of the largest U.S. chemical companies, Dow and DuPont, had stopped developing PBB in 1970. Research had indicated that the product might have toxic effects and that it might build up in the environment. In spite of these findings, industrial demand for PBB was still growing. Manufacturers combined it with other compounds to produce nonflammable plastic casings for hi-fi components, radios, and television sets.

At Michigan Chemical, the trade name for PBB was Firemaster. The highly toxic, brown crystals were packaged in 50-pound (22.68-kg) brown bags, and these bags, too, had the name of the product clearly stenciled across the front.

Both Nutrimaster and Firemaster were stacked near each other at the factory in the spring of 1973. Somehow—nobody can tell how it happened—a few bags of Firemaster were included in a shipment of Nutrimaster to the Michigan Farm Services cattle feed-mixing plant.

Because magnesium oxide was so popular with dairy farmers that year, operators at the mixing plant had been seeing a lot of it. It came from several different factories, in many kinds of wrappings, and under several brand names. They liked to keep it all together in one spot near the mixing machines. There, in June of 1973, operators noticed bags stamped with what appeared to be two different brand names for magnesium oxide, standing side by side: Nutrimaster and Firemaster. As they were taking stock, they listed the two together. They also used them together.

It is not certain just how many bags of PBB were actually added to the feed of Michigan dairy herds during the next eight or nine months. Investigators later guessed that it must have been between ten and twenty 50-pound (22.68-kg) bags.

The wasting disease crept up on the cattle. For many agonized months, farmers met only scorn and criticism when they attempted to get help. Outsiders questioned their farming skills and suggested that they must be starving their cattle or feeding them moldy grain. Yet it was plain enough that something deadly was at work. Farm cats and kittens, frequent visitors to the milking pails, died in great numbers, and so did the mice and rats in the barns.

More trouble awaited the farmers when scientists finally found out what was poisoning the herds. PBB (polybrominated biphenyl) is a chemical relative of PCB (polychlorinated biphenyl) and has the same tendency to enter the fatty tissues of the body and to accumulate there. Officials of the Department of Agriculture wanted to prevent the milk and meat of contaminated cattle from being sent to market. They placed all farms that reported sick cattle in quarantine. The owners of these farms could do only one thing: pour out their milk and bury their cows.

Because the cows were sick and dying from
the effects of PBBs, many Michigan farmers were
forced to destroy entire herds of cattle in 1975.

For many farmers quarantine would have meant financial ruin. So, instead of reporting their sick cows they chose to keep quiet about them and to keep on selling milk, butter, and cheese. As for the animals that no longer gave milk, the farmers sent them to market to be slaughtered for meat.

Altogether, it was too late for quarantine to stop the spreading of PBB throughout Michigan and even beyond. As many as 100,000 heavily contaminated animals had gone to market during the ten or twelve months before the accident was discovered. Beef, milk, butter, and cheese were not the only contaminated products. Chicken feed, too, was mixed and processed at the farm cooperative, and the dust of PBB had penetrated every crevice of the machinery. Waste meat products from slaughterhouses were, as usual, processed and converted into protein feed pellets for flocks of chickens, turkeys, and geese. Thus, the poison traveled throughout the food chain. By 1975, PBB contamination had spread to hogs and sheep as well as poultry and eggs.

PBB is extremely persistent. At the Farm Bureau's feed plant, repeated clean-up efforts were largely unsuccessful. Traces of the toxin were found in scoops, bins, grinders, buckets, mixers, floor cracks and even on ceiling beams and on the loading docks. Nine hundred tons of feed were destroyed. But by then, unknown quantities had been consumed.

Scientists are not sure if PBB is carcinogenic to humans. In laboratory experiments, mice on a PBB diet have developed an unusually high number of tumors. More time must pass, though, before all the results of several studies give us definite answers.

We do know for sure that, in 1978, 90 percent of the people living in Michigan had PBB in their blood. We also know that contaminated foods from Michigan were sold and eaten in at least thirteen other states.

TOXIC FOODS
An accidental contaminant that turns up in food more and more often is PBB's chemical relative, the worldwide toxic

substance, PCB. In 1979, Department of Agriculture inspectors found PCB in animal feed in seventeen states, coast to coast. As a result, thousands of pounds of pork and poultry, as well as 73,000 pounds (33,100 kg) of various contaminated egg products had to be kept from going to market.

According to the Office of Technological Assessment in Washington, low-level poisons of many kinds frequently enter the public food supply. More often than not, these accidents go unreported. Some cases of poisoning take years to build up and to be discovered. Others, perhaps, have only a slight impact and receive no public attention. Even so, the agency was called upon to study 243 cases of accidental food contamination in just two years, between 1976 and 1978.

CHEMICALS ON THE FARM
Altogether, farming today is a highly polluting industry. We tend to think that farmers work in wholesome surroundings where air and water are fresh and unspoiled. Actually, the contrary is more likely to be true. A 1971–1978 study of the death certificates of more than twenty thousand Iowa farmers (women and blacks were not included in the study) showed that six types of cancer occurred far more often in these men than in city dwellers. Only lung cancer had affected the group at a lower rate, apparently because Iowa farmers, on the whole, tend to avoid tobacco.

The reasons for this high cancer rate are not clear. What we do know is that the use of chemicals is essential to a modern farm. Crop dusting—the pesticide spraying of fields and orchards by plane—is an obvious source of air pollution in the countryside. Less obvious is the way in which pesticides used on farmlands seep into the ground water reservoirs, the aquifers, that supply a region's springs and wells.

ASBESTOS
The ancient Romans combined the crumbly white fibers of asbestos with colored threads and wove them into magnificent garments. Even then, observers noticed that workers

who handled asbestos were apt to develop a strange and usually fatal lung disease.

All the same, asbestos retained its uses throughout the centuries. It was not only valued for its light weight and whiteness, but more especially for its resistance to heat and fire. It could be spun into cloth, pressed into paper, whipped into a fire-smothering spray, combined with cement and plaster, or mixed with hundreds of other materials to make them fire resistant. It became especially valuable in the age of electrical appliances, all of which must be protected by insulation.

Every American home today is likely to contain dozens of asbestos products. Even without counting the electrical and heating appliances we are likely to come across asbestos in such products as protective shielding for hot water pipes, floor and ceiling tiles, ironing board covers, pot holders, carpet padding, movie screens, roofing shingles, caulk and putty, sprayed insulation, paints, varnishes, plaster, and even phonograph records. Asbestos is also a staple in automobile production where it is highly prized for use in body filler, brake linings, undercoating, and insulation.

In some of these products asbestos fibers are firmly locked into the material. In others, though, they are loose and crumbly, disintegrating into fine dust at a touch. When the tiny, loose fibers are inhaled, they work themselves into the lungs and remain there to cause three possible diseases: asbestosis, a clogging of the lungs that eventually prevents breathing; cancer of the lungs; and mesothelioma, a cancer of the lining of the lungs or abdominal wall, which kills within a few months after symptoms are first discovered. All these diseases develop slowly, sometimes over a span of twenty to thirty years after first exposure.

In recent decades, architects thought of asbestos as a practical and decorative solution to the hazard of fire in public buildings. Beginning in the 1930s, builders developed a new technique for spraying asbestos mixed with plaster on walls and ceilings, and freely used this technique in constructing new schools. After ten or twenty years, though, these walls tend to deteriorate. A fine dust is released to sift down over children and teachers.

Experience with shipyard workers employed in asbestos spraying during World War II has shown how deadly such contact can be. These workers later became a prey to the specific lung diseases caused by inhaling asbestos fibers. Because of this unhappy discovery, the EPA, in 1973, banned spray applications of any material containing more than 1 percent asbestos in weight. Since then, several communities across the United States have closed schools which have crumbling asbestos walls.

In the spring of 1979, the EPA prepared an information package telling school personnel how to take samples of crumbling plaster and how to analyze them for asbestos fibers. As with other inhaled particles that remain permanently in the lungs, the effects of asbestos are aggravated by smoking. A teacher who works in an asbestos-contaminated building and also smokes tends to increase his or her risk of developing lung cancer by 50 percent.

FLUOROCARBONS

Spray cans were among the many convenient new gadgets of the postwar era. There was something highly satisfying in the ease with which they worked at a touch of the finger. Manufacturers marketed one product after another in this successful form. Perfumes and paints, laundry starch, bug-killers, and furniture wax, all came out in spray cans.

The aerosol gases that propel the spray out of the can seemed to be wonderfully safe and efficient. They are highly stable, which means that they do not react with other substances and are, therefore, neither poisonous nor flammable. Fluorocarbons are more properly called chlorofluoromethanes. As the name implies, these synthetic gases are composed of chlorine and fluorine atoms attached to the carbon atom in methane.

The fluorocarbons have several important uses. As refrigerants in air conditioners and refrigerators they work so well that no other chemical can really replace them. They are also used to blow the millions of small bubbles that give body to plastic foam, both the rigid and the bouncy kinds.

As more and more people demanded air conditioners, not only in public places but also in their homes and cars, vast quantities of fluorocarbons were manufactured. Plastic foam, too, became increasingly popular for everything from ice buckets to armchairs. Then, in the early 1970s, consumers and manufacturers received another unpleasant surprise. Scientists had discovered that, once released, fluorocarbons slowly rise to the earth's upper atmosphere. There, the sun's energy breaks down the gases and frees the chlorine atoms. These chlorine atoms begin a chain reaction that destroys the layer of ozone which protects the earth from the sun's deadly ultraviolet rays. If we earth dwellers continue to release fluorocarbons, we will gradually deplete the protective shield that envelops our globe.

Experts warned that hundreds of thousands of additional skin cancers could result in the United States alone. They warned of increased risks of melanoma, a skin cancer that is often quick and fatal. Biologists expressed their concern for possible changes in plant growth. Photosynthesis, the way in which plants convert carbon dioxide into oxygen with the aid of sunlight, might be affected. Marine biologists worried about possible effects on phytoplankton, the tiny organisms that nourish ocean life. Finally, meteorologists warned that the thinning of the ozone shield could permanently change the earth's climate.

At first, most people found it hard to believe that using such a harmless-looking object as a spray can could result in widespread devastation. For four years, no action was taken. Finally, in May 1977, the United States placed a ban on fluorocarbon spray propellants but allowed existing quantities to be sold for two more years.

Meanwhile, though, experts took stock of other uses of fluorocarbons. One fourth of the total output is used in refrigerants, where no good substitute has yet been found. Another quarter of the total is used in making paint solvents and plastics. Some of these uses are not essential. Others, though, cannot be eliminated at present.

Recently, several scientific organizations have repeated their urgent warning. New measurements have not only confirmed the earlier estimates of the danger but have found it to be even greater. If the use of fluorocarbons keeps on growing without severe restrictions, the world's ozone layer may be reduced by 13 percent. Half of this reduction would probably occur within the next fifty years.

Fluorocarbons take decades to reach the stratosphere some 15 to 20 miles (24.0 to 32.0 km) away from earth. Because they travel so slowly, it is hard to say how much damage has already been done. In 1980, though, medical reports from regions in California told of an increasing number of melanoma cases and other skin cancers from causes that have not been determined.

CHAPTER X
ACTION

Ignorance, greed, and wasteful management have done great harm to our surroundings. Can we have a flourishing technology and still conserve nature? This disturbing, complex problem has no easy solution. Tough work lies ahead for the minds and hands of our day. Clearly, we must take stock, set up rules, and try to save the earth from further damage.

MONITORING

In the wake of a mountain storm, five backpackers drenched in sweat and rainwater are struggling upward through dense forest. These young men and women are part of a monitoring and sampling team of the EPA-National Park Service. Right now they are working in Great Smokies National Park. Their aim is to check on earlier findings of lead pollution in the mountains. They halt at a clearing from which warm mist is rising. Out of their blue and orange packs come gauges, meters, wires. Quickly, with expert hands, they set up their air-quality monitoring equipment. They assemble it in a teepee-like structure and surround it with a few protective loops of barbed wire. Young bears are curious and apt to knock over instruments with a stroke of their paw. Before climbing to their next station, the team members put on plastic gloves and carefully collect a few samples of plants, soil, and rainwater, for study in the laboratory.

At about the same time, on the eastern coast of the United States, a dozen bright-hooded figures in hip boots are sloshing across a tract of Long Island marsh. Led by their professor, these students from the nearby State Agricultural and Technical College are keeping track of contamination affecting one of the island's most precious resources. The students stop to measure the water temperature of a small stream that crosses the wetlands. Later, in a trailer-truck equipped as a laboratory, they will assess water samples they have taken, measuring oxygen level, acidity, and bacteria content.

In California, the Scripps Institute of Oceanography supervises yet another of the many monitoring activities conducted all over America. Here, it is Project Musselwatch. For this project, researchers collect samples of mussels and oysters from one hundred coastal stations and systematically analyze them for toxic compounds. Shellfish take in such compounds with their nourishment and store them in their muscle tissues. This makes them good indicators of pollution levels in U.S. coastal waters.

ANTI-POLLUTION TECHNOLOGY

Monitoring alone, of course, is not enough. Where pollution has occurred, technology must devise new ways to do things. First of all, research departments of colleges and universities, government agencies, and private companies are working to develop new and safe sources of energy, such as fusion and solar power. They are also concentrating on reducing the damage done to air and water by coal burning plants. One such project, sponsored by the Department of Energy, is in formation at the University of Buffalo. Scientists there are perfecting a technique for using very intense sound waves to make coal smoke particles stick to one another and form an inert mass that can be collected with the coal ash.

MODERN DISPOSAL TECHNIQUES

In the future, waste disposal will never again be a matter of simple "dumping." Several techniques are gaining widespread use. One way to destroy many hazardous wastes is to burn them at ultra-high temperatures. Another technique is to solidify liquids and encase them in metal. The containers can then be buried, preferably in a dry space, far underground.

The waste disposal business is booming. Some of the foremost disposal companies have developed million dollar showcase facilities using burial methods far advanced over those used years ago in the Love Canal. A modern secure landfill site, as approved by the EPA, is usually a huge clay basin, its bottom at least 50 feet (15 m) thick, and resting on solid bedrock. It is equipped with a drainage system, gas venting system and monitoring wells for inspecting the contents. It includes a waste water treatment plant to process any toxic leakage. The waste containers are stacked inside this basin over a system of pipes resting on a bed of gravel. Finally they are covered with successive layers of clay, polyethelene, sand, and more clay.

Before disposal, company chemists analyze the wastes that will be accepted for burial. Workers separate shipments on arrival to prevent contact between those that might react with one another. If wastes are liquid, they are turned into paste before being packed into drums.

After burial, the wastes remain under continual surveillance. To protect customers from any legal claims, high priced liability insurance is one of the services these companies offer.

CLEAN-UP COSTS

For most manufacturers, cleaning up their operations is bound to be costly. When industries install air scrubbers or water filters, when they use modern disposal plants and incinerators for their wastes, or when they transport these wastes a long distance away for disposal, they do indeed incur extra expense. Some manufacturers help themselves by selling their products at a higher price. Others are afraid that the expenditure of cleaning up will drive them out of business. But even though economists predict that waste control and cleaning of contaminated areas will cost industry hundreds of billions of dollars each year, the destruction caused by uncontrolled industrial pollution would be even costlier.

Actually, research has shown that cleaner air and water can actually prove to be an economic benefit. In one study of time and wages lost because of illness due to smog pollution, economists estimated that a 60 percent reduction in pollution level would result in benefits of $36 billion a year. This study does not even consider such other losses due to air pollution as corrosion of building materials and paint, lowered crop yield on farms, destruction of trees and garden plants, and death of sweet-water fish.

In fact, environmental considerations tend to force only the oldest, most poorly equipped industries to close down. Antipollution laws do not create unemployment. On the contrary: jobs are created by new industries producing waste recycling fixtures and pollution control devices. In 1978, EPA administrators estimated that the agency's multi-billion-dollar waste water treatment plant construction program had created ninety-five thousand jobs across the nation. Altogether, some 700,000 men and women are directly employed in pollution control. Not all these people are scientists and engineers. Some of them work as skilled operators, technicians, clerical employees, and unskilled laborers.

SLOW PROGRESS

From 1980 on, all manufacturers of hazardous materials are required by the EPA to designate exactly where they will dispose of every single waste shipment. The document of disposal must be signed by the transporter and by the owner of the site before it is returned again to the sender. The government hopes that this will prevent illegal dumping in mine shafts, ditches, rivers, and sewers. It will be difficult, though, to find several hundred new legal disposal sites. Most communities do not want these depositories near them.

To cope with existing pollution, the EPA has asked Congress to approve a multi-million-dollar clean-up fund, known as a superfund, to which the chemical industry will eventually be asked to contribute a major share.

Above all, the Environmental Protection Agency is trying to establish human tolerance levels for many toxic substances that have never before been controlled. Once legal standards are set, industries that exceed permitted limits can be prosecuted.

Recently, several environmental groups have accused the EPA of being far too slow and indecisive in regulating industry. The facts of the matter, though, are complicated. The industries, indeed, wish to avoid controls and have responded by evasion, pleas of hardship, or lawsuits and countersuits. Then, too, the number of substances possibly to be placed under control is immense. Finally, as one government representative recently put it, there are still no absolute scientific criteria agreed upon as to adequate testing methods for setting safety standards. As yet, toxicology is something of an art form rather than a science.

TRASH AND TREASURE

In a complex economy, trash can sometimes turn into treasure. The waste products of one industry might well serve as the raw materials for another. Large steel mills sell ammonia and tar which are simply waste products from the steel plant's own coke manufacturing process. Of course, the problem here is to make sure the "waste" product to be sold has been purified of other industrial contaminants. In Europe, there have long been waste exchanges to coordinate the buying and selling of material that would otherwise be considered hazardous trash with a high price tag on its removal. Recently, a similar exchange program has been started by the Missouri Department of Natural Resources. It is the first American clearing house for materials that pose difficult disposal problems.

Because the future of nuclear energy in the United States is now uncertain, no one can predict what will be done with the high-level wastes of spent nuclear fuel. France, England, and the Soviet Union, though, have built facilities for recycling spent fuel not only for use by their own power plants but also for export abroad.

COOPERATION

Pollution does not respect state lines or national borders. Until now, much environmental damage has gone uncorrected because official boundary lines place the source of pollution and its victims under two different judicial systems. More cooperation is needed between the United States and our neighbors—Canada to the north, and Mexico to the south—to prevent mutual contamination of the air and water we share.

Rivalry between communities, between federal, state, and local agencies, or between different departments of the federal government is another reason for delays in cleaning up industrial pollution. One major repository of nuclear wastes for example, has long been an object of controversy between several U.S. senators and representatives. Each of them is sponsoring a different bill for dealing with the radioactive waste situation. All agree the federal government should take over responsibility for the site from the state of New York. How should it be done, though? That's the question. The nuclear wastes have been stored in a tank at the closed nuclear reprocessing plant for the last ten years. Until now, the tank has shown no signs of leaking. Yet, time may be running out and, meanwhile, each political rival's bill is blocking the passage of the others.

Finally, industrial countries will have to be more responsible for coping with their own waste products instead of trying to foist them on others. International waste disposal companies, searching for places to bury hazardous materials, are eager to buy dumping sites in industrially undeveloped areas, such as parts of Africa, for example. The price for unused land is often very tempting to small nations without sizable revenues. Yet many of these countries now have the foresight to refuse becoming a receptacle for toxic wastes created abroad.

A MEASURE OF SUCCESS

You are probably wondering what each of us can do about contaminated air, water, and food. First of all, it is important to be aware of the dangers. Read labels before buying. Handle materials with care. Store things safely. Gloves and masks are available for those who have to work with hazardous products. Various filters can be obtained for improving unsafe drinking water, although caution must be exercised here because water filters must be well engineered to be truly effective.

One rather simple way for people in almost any community to nurse their surroundings back to health is to plant trees or tall hedges. Greenbelts such as tree-lined streets, gardens, parks, and forests, all serve as powerful anti-pollution buffers. They reduce heat, noise, and glare, filter out dust, and block odors of gasoline exhaust.

A recent study revealed that a two-and-a-half-acre stand of beech trees could remove sixty-eight tons of dust from the air. In another experiment, a dense hedgerow prevented 40 percent of the lead content in the air from filtering through to the other side. Plants and their soil absorb noxious sulfer dioxide, ozone, hydrocarbons, and carbon monoxide. Parks are life savers in big cities. Hyde Park, in the center of London, reduces the concentration of smoke by about 27 percent.

Remember that many environmental rescue projects have been entirely successful. A striking example is that of Jamaica Bay, only 15 miles (24.0 km) outside of New York City. For decades, Jamaica Bay served New York's industries and homes as garbage dump and sewer outlet. It became an ill-smelling desert, piled with trash, the hunting ground of rats.

Then a Parks Department employee thought of planting a few trees. The results were encouraging and soon the city supported the rehabilitation of the area. Marsh grass began to grow after New York sewers were diverted to water treatment plants instead of running directly into the bay. Shellfish and fin fish began to return, and water birds came back in great numbers and varieties. Today, Jamaica Bay is the bird sanctuary receiving the largest number of birds on the East Coast, even though it is near Kennedy International Airport where jets never stop zooming in and out.

Not every pollution story has such a happy ending, though, especially not where long-lived chemicals are concerned. At the Love Canal site, of course, grass grew only sparsely; the trees people planted cracked the clay covering the chemicals underground, and soon all vegetation died. We know, then, that to refresh our world we will have to work on many different fronts. We will have to plan better, cooperate more closely, and show greater discipline and economy in using natural resources and energy.

Above all, we will need science and technology more than ever. From now on, though, it will have to be science and technology with a conscience.

FOR
FURTHER READING

Asimov, Isaac. *Earth: Our Crowded Spaceship.* New York: The John Day Company, 1974.

Berger, Melvin. *Pollution Lab: Scientists at Work.* New York: The John Day Company, 1974.

Brown, Joseph E. *Oil Spills: Danger in the Sea.* New York: Dodd, Mead and Company, 1978.

Brown, Michael H. *Laying Waste: The Poisoning of America by Toxic Chemicals.* New York: Pantheon Books, 1980.

Chen, Edwin. *PBB: An American Tragedy.* Englewood Cliffs, N.J.: Prentice-Hall, 1979.

Elliott, Sarah M. *Our Dirty Land.* New York: Julian Messner, 1976.

Fagan, John J. *The Earth Environment.* Englewood Cliffs, N.J.: Prentice-Hall, 1974.

Fuller, John. *The Poison That Fell from the Sky.* New York: Random House, 1977.

Grant, Neil. *The Industrial Revolution.* New York: Franklin Watts, 1973.

Whiteside, Thomas. *The Pendulum and the Toxic Cloud.* New Haven: Yale University Press, 1977.

INDEX

117]